The Story of Original Sin

The Story of Original Sin

JOHN E. TOEWS

☙PICKWICK *Publications* · Eugene, Oregon

THE STORY OF ORIGINAL SIN

Pickwick Publications
An Imprint of Wipf and Stock Publishers
199 W. 8th Ave., Suite 3
Eugene, OR 97401

www.wipfandstock.com

ISBN 13: 978-1-62032-369-4

Cataloguing-in-Publication Data

Toews, John E., 1937–.

The story of original sin / John E. Toews.

xii + 132 p. ; 23 cm. Includes bibliographical references and index.

ISBN 13: 978-1-55635-985-9

1. Sin, Original—History of doctrines. 2. Sin—Christianity—History of Doctrines. I. Title.

BT715 T64 2013

To Arlene, my devoted wife of fifty-four years; and our son Mark, a bio-chemist by training, who encouraged me repeatedly to write this book out of our numerous conversations about the problematic of the traditional Western Christian understanding of sin.

Contents

Acknowledgments

THIS BOOK, LIKE MOST, is the product of conversations, first with students over forty-five years of teaching who found the Western Christian doctrine of original sin problematic, and then especially with our son Mark, who found the doctrine scientifically untenable.

I am profoundly grateful for friends and colleagues who read drafts of the manuscript and gave me feedback—Mark Baker, professor of theology at the Fresno Pacific University Biblical Seminary; Al Dueck, professor of the integration of psychology and theology at Fuller Theological Seminary; Abe Friesen, professor emeritus of reformation studies at the University of California, Santa Barbara; Lynn Jost, Vice-President and professor of Old Testament at Fresno Pacific University Biblical Seminary; William Klassen, former faculty at Associated Mennonite Seminaries, the University of Manitoba, who also taught at Simon Fraser University, the University of Toronto, the Ecole Biblique in Jerusalem, served as the Dean of the Ecumenical Institute in Jerusalem and is the Principal Emeritus of St. Paul's College at the University of Waterloo; Elmer Martens, former president and professor emeritus of Old Testament at Fresno Pacific University Biblical Seminary; Ryan Schellenberg, assistant professor of biblical studies at Fresno Pacific University; Peter Smith, assistant professor of peace and conflict studies at Fresno Pacific University; Delbert Wiens, professor emeritus of ancient history and classical studies at Fresno Pacific University. Their feedback was helpful, but they bear no responsibility for any errors in the book.

I also am very grateful for the help of Hope Nisly, Ernest Carrere, and Anne Guenther, all staff in the Hiebert Library of Fresno Pacific University. They expanded the collection of a relatively small library by purchasing books that I needed, or pointed me to materials I had overlooked, or ordered numerous books and journal articles from libraries across North America via inter-library loan.

The librarians at the University of California Merced, especially Tyler, deserve thanks for helping me access the Patrologia Graeca and Patrologia Latina via the web.

It has been a privilege to work with the staff of Wipf and Stock, especially Christian Amondson, Robin Parry, and Ian Creeger. They have been gracious, prompt, and have a wonderful eye for detail.

Abbreviations

AB   *Anchor Bible*. Edited by William Foxwell Albright and David Noel Freedman. New York: Doubleday, 1956–.

ABD   *The Anchor Bible Dictionary*. 6 vols. Edited by David Noel Freedman. New York: Doubleday, 1992.

ANF   *Ante-Nicene Fathers*. 9 vols. Edited by Alexander Roberts and James Donaldson. Reprint. Peabody, MA: Hendrickson, 1999.

JBL   *Journal of Biblical Literature*

JSNTS   *Journal for the Study of the New Testament*

NIDB   *New Interpreters Dictionary of the Bible*. 6 vols. Edited by Katherine D. Sakenfeld. Nashville: Abingdon, 2009.

NIDOTTE   *New International Dictionary of Old Testament Theology and Exegesis*. 5 vols. Edited by William A. Van Gemeren. Grand Rapids: Zondervan, 1997.

NIDNTT   *New International Dictionary of New Testament Theology*. 3 vols. Edited by Colin Brown. Zondervan, 1975, 1976, 1978.

NPNF   *Nicene and Post-Nicene Fathers*. 14 vols. Edited by Philip Schaff. Peabody, MA: Hendrickson, 2004.

OTP   *The Old Testament Pseudepigrapha*. 2 vols. Edited by James H. Charlesworth. Garden City, NY: Doubleday, 1983, 1985.

SNTMS   Society of New Testament Monograph Series. Cambridge: Cambridge University Press.

TDOT   *Theological Dictionary of the Old Testament.* 13 vols. Edited by G. Johannes Botterweck and Helmer Ringgren. Grand Rapids: Eerdmans, 1974–77.

TDNT   *Theological Dictionary of the New Testament.* 10 vols. Edited by Gerhard Kittel and Gerhard Friedrich. Grand Rapids: Eerdmans, 1964–76.

Introduction

GARY ANDERSON SAYS THAT "sin has a history."[1] That is, there is a story behind the theology of sin. The thesis of this book is that there is a story behind the theology of original sin, and that the history of that story by the time we reach its classical formulation in Augustine in the late fourth and early fifth century is a long way from the beginning of the story in the narrative of Genesis 3.

I grew up in a conservative evangelical home and community in which I was taught that I was "born in sin." That is, I was a sinner from birth, and, therefore, I needed to repent of my sin and put my faith in Jesus Christ in order to be forgiven of my inherited or original sin plus the sins I had committed as a child growing up. I did as I was taught, and at a young age in a revival meeting in which the evangelist frightened me with a graphic sermon on the horrors of hell, I repented of my sin/sins and confessed my faith in Jesus as my Savior.

The general teaching in the Mennonite Brethren Church of which I became a member, the Christian high school which I attended, the Christian liberal arts college which I attended all reaffirmed in general terms the doctrine of original sin. It was not until my senior year in college that I received specific teaching about the theology of original sin. In a course entitled "The Essentials of Christianity" taught by J. B. Toews, my father, I was required to read Eric Sauer's *The Dawn of World Redemption* and Augustus H. Strong's *Systematic Theology*. From Sauer I learned that Satan had been a prince or viceroy of God who had rebelled against God and been expelled from the heavenly court, although Sauer admitted that there was no biblical evidence for this understanding.[2] This Satan was responsible for the temptation of Eve and "the fall" of Adam and Eve.

---

1. Anderson, *Sin*, 6.

2. Sauer, *Redemption*, 32–34.

Because Adam was the organic representative of "mankind," "the fall" was universal and "death established itself upon all his descendants."[3] Every individual was "in Adam."[4]

Strong articulated the same theology but with different language. The context for the discussion of original sin was the law. Adam's sin in the Garden was the violation of the law.[5] Adam's sin was "imputed to all his posterity so that "in Adam all die."[6] Strong explicitly embraced a theology of sin articulated by a church father named Augustine in the mid-390s and early 400s: "God imputes the sin of Adam immediately to all his posterity, in virtue of that organic unity of mankind by which the whole race at the time of Adam's transgression existed, not individually, but seminally, in him as its head. The total life of humanity was then in Adam; the race as yet had its being only in him. In Adam's free act, the will of the race revolted from God and the nature of the race corrupted itself."[7] Traducianism is the theory of sin transmission that Strong embraced; that is, in the sexual act, the male transmits sin through the sperm that fertilizes the female egg. The result is that all of Adam's posterity is born into the same state into which Adam fell, that is, total depravity. All humans are born with the complete corruption of their moral nature and a bias toward evil.[8]

The Virgin Birth of Jesus, we were told in class, was necessary to remove the male from the reproductive cycle in order to stop the transmission of sin.

It seemed a little strange to me, so I recall pressing my father at home. He told me that Strong had been the textbook he had virtually memorized in the theology classes with Professor H. W. Lohrenz as a new immigrant student from Russia at Tabor College in Hillsboro, Kansas, in the 1930s. He assured me the same theology was taught at Western Theological Seminary in Portland, Oregon, where he earned his Th.M. in 1940 and at Southwestern Theological Seminary in Dallas, Texas, where he pursued doctoral studies in theology in the mid-1940s. It was the orthodox understanding of sin and the basis for the orthodox interpretation of the atonement of Christ, he said.

3. Ibid., 56.
4. Ibid., 56–57.
5. Strong, *Theology*, 533f.
6. Ibid., 593.
7. Ibid., 619.
8. Ibid., 637f.

To use theological language, I was taught as a young Christian and a college student that sin was an ontological reality, that I was sinful by nature apart from any choice or action of my choosing. Sin defined my being from the moment of conception. There was nothing that I could do about it because my nature, my being had been corrupted by Adam's sin in the Garden.

One man many centuries ago determined how my church, and most Protestant, and all Catholic churches understood sin. And that understanding shaped the churches theologies of salvation. How could one man have so much influence? How could he have so much influence especially when I had difficulty finding his theology supported by my reading of the Bible? But, then I did not know Hebrew and Greek at the time. I checked some other evangelical books on theology, and they all seemed to agree with my father, Eric Sauer, and A. H. Strong. But I remained unpersuaded. The traducian theory of sin transmission via sexual intercourse seemed especially farfetched. The explanation of the Virgin Birth as necessary to remove the male from the reproductive process really seemed strange. I thought Jesus was to be exactly like us in order to redeem us, but now suddenly he was very different from us. Was I alone in wondering about these things?

My doctoral studies in New Testament made me very aware of how history puts glasses on the way we read and understand biblical texts. My study of early church history and literature (patristics) helped me realize the paradigmatic effect on biblical interpretation of people like Constantine and Augustine. In my early study of Romans I saw a disconnect between what Paul said about sin in Romans 5:12 and what Augustine said about the meaning of Romans 5:12, but I did not have the time or the courage as a young teacher in the church to address the issue openly; I would whisper to my students that there were problems they might want to explore. I would occasionally hear or read scholars say Augustine's doctrine of original sin was not biblical (e.g., James McClendon),[9] but they did not support these claims with a study of the critical biblical texts or trace the history of the emergence of the doctrine. This book tries to do what I found missing, to carefully trace the history of the interpretation of Genesis 3 that led to the formulation of the doctrine of original of sin.

9. Strong, *Theology*, 125.

1

The Story of Sin in Genesis 3

THE STORY OF SIN begins in Genesis 3. The present form of Genesis 3 is dated between the tenth century BCE[1] to Israel's exile (587–537 BCE).[2] There is widespread agreement that it is written in a very literary, even poetic style, and with great rhetorical skill and nuance.[3]

It is important to note at the outset that the word "sin" is not used in Genesis 3 nor is the word "original sin" used in the story, or anywhere in the Bible. The form of Genesis 3 is a crime and punishment narrative that is told in two parts: 1) the transgression, vv. 1–7, and 2) the punishment, vv. 8–24.

THE TRANSGRESSION, VV. 1–7

The story of the transgression is told in three parts: 1) the temptation, vv. 1–5; 2) the transgression, v. 6; 3) the change effected by the transgression, v. 7.

1. So Wenham, *Genesis 1–15*, xlii–xlv.

2. So Bruggemann, *Introduction*, 5, 21.

3. See Trible, *God and Rhetoric*, 72–143.

The temptation,

The temptation, vv. 1–5, is initiated by "the serpent" (*arum*). The only thing we know about the serpent is that it "was more crafty than any other wild animal that the Lord God had made" (v. 1). So the serpent is one of the "animals of the field" formed out of the ground by the Lord God (2:19). In addition, the text says that it talks (v. 1), and that it knows something that humans do not know (v. 5). The text says nothing about the serpent as Satan or as some kind of demonic figure, nor anything about enmity between the serpent and God. The serpent is introduced in the story because of what it says, not because of who or what it is. The man and woman are led into disobedience by a creature of God. The story in Genesis tells us nothing about any fallen angel, Satan, or the origin of evil.[4]

The serpent initiates a pious dialogue, what Dietrich Bonhoeffer called "the first conversation about God, the first religious, theological conversation."[5] The opening question is, "did God say . . .?" The serpent exaggerates God's prohibition by asking, "did God say, 'you shall not eat from any tree in the garden'"(3:2)? The woman (she is not given a name, Eve, until v. 20) corrects the serpent's exaggeration, "you shall not eat of the fruit of the tree that is in the middle of the garden," but then offers her own exaggeration, "nor shall you touch it, or you shall die" (3:3). The serpent challenges the credibility of God, "you will not die. . ." but "your eyes will be opened, and you will be like God (or the gods), knowing good and evil" (3:4). You will see what until now you are not able to perceive, and you will be made wise (or successful) to distinguish what is useful or harmful for the community.[6] At the conclusion of the dialogue the issue is can God be trusted? Has God been completely truthful with humans? A pious question about God is really a very cunning question because it forces the woman to render a judgment about God.

It is important to note here that "to know good and evil" (v. 4) is a leitmotif in the narrative; it occurs four times in chapters 2–3 (2:9, 17; 3:5, 22). A study of these occurrences indicates that 1) the prediction that "you will die" is disputed: God predicts it in 2:17, the serpent challenges

---

4. The association of the serpent and Satan begins in Wisdom 2:24 (written in the first decades of the Common Era, or about the time of the Apostle Paul). See Fretheim, "Genesis 3 a Fall Story?" 149–51; Fretheim, *Genesis*, 359–60; Brown, "Devil in the Details," 200–227; Russell, *The Devil*, 174–220; and Kelly, *Satan*, 13–113.

5. Bonhoeffer, *Creation and Fall*, 111.

6. See von Rad, *Genesis*, 89; and Westermann, *Genesis 1–11*, 240–48 for this communal understanding.

it in 3:5, neither the woman nor Adam die in the account. 2) The phrase "your eyes will be opened" (3:4, 7) describes the process by which Adam and the woman come to the knowledge of good and evil. 3) The phrase "you will be like God" or "the gods" (3:5, 22) describes the ability to know good and evil.

The transgression

The transgression, v. 6, occurs in two movements. The woman sees that the tree is aesthetically attractive—it appeals to the sense of sight and taste—and that it is to be desired to make one wise. The text is restrained and nuanced. The desire is for wisdom, for the possibility to transcend one's limitations by gaining new knowledge and insight. There is no hint in the text of desire that leads to passion that leads to sex, as Augustine interpreted it, and then added that such desire and its accompanying passion and sex was sinful. The text also does not say that the woman wanted to become "like God," although that is generally the way it has been interpreted since Ambrosiaster and Augustine in the late fourth and early fifth centuries CE.

The transgression in v. 6 is that the woman ate the fruit because she desired to become wise.[7]

The second movement in the text is that the woman "also gave some to her husband," who "was with her (*immah*)," and "he ate." Adam was not tempted; he was beside the woman the whole time and simply conformed to her behavior. The text does not suggest that the woman was more susceptible to temptation than the man and that after being tempted she became the man's temptress.[8]

What was the transgression, the "primal sin"? The serpent asked the woman and Adam to make a judgment about God. They did. They both, standing together, decided to mistrust God, to mistrust the word of God, in quest for autonomy that would make them wise. Their mistrust of God led them to disobedience, to disobey the word of God.[9]

---

7. It is important to note that the text does not say that the fruit of the tree was an apple; that designation reflects the later understanding of Latin Christianity.

8. See Trible, *God and Rhetoric*, 113.

9. See Biddle, *Missing the Mark*, 12–13, 75–94, for a very good discussion of the transgression in this text as mistrust and sin as mistrust more generally in the Scriptures.

The Change Effected by the Transgression

The change effected by the transgression, v. 7, is narrated in three events: 1) their eyes are opened—they see what they had not seen before; 2) they see that they are naked (*arummim*, a play on the word *arum*, "crafty, prudent," used in 3:1); 3) they sew fig leaves to cover their nakedness.

The effect of eating the fruit of "the knowledge of good and evil" was that Adam and the woman were changed, as the serpent had predicted. They did not die, but they were changed. They see the world differently. The nature of the changed perspective is enigmatic. In 2:24 they become one flesh; that is, they consummated the relationship in sexual intercourse. In 2:25 they are naked and not ashamed, which, as Gordon Wenham points out, is best translated as "they were unabashed" or "they were not disconcerted" just like little children are unashamed of their nakedness.[10] But in 3:7 they suddenly realize that it is not appropriate to be naked and they cover themselves. Or, to use gender language, in 2:25 they see each other naked and do not notice their gender, but in 3:7 they suddenly realize that they are gendered, that they are sexually different. Something profound has changed by the eating of the fruit.[11]

THE PUNISHMENT, VV. 8-24

The punishment for Adam and the woman eating the forbidden fruit is expulsion from the garden. God put Adam and the woman in the garden. Adam and the woman chose to mistrust and, therefore, to disobey God. God expelled them from the garden. The explicit reason for the expulsion, stated in v. 22, is to prevent Adam and the woman from reaching out and taking fruit "from the tree of life, and eat, and live forever."[12]

The serpent said that Adam and the woman would die if they disobeyed God. But they did not. Some commentators and preachers have asked if the serpent told the truth while God lied? But, let's remember the text was written with great literary skill and nuance. V. 8 describes "God walking in the garden . . ." The word "walking" is used in the Hebrew Scriptures of God's presence among God's people, especially in the sanctuary (e.g., Lev 26:12; Deut 23:15; 2 Sam 7:6–7). In addition, many scholars have noted similarities between features of the Garden and the Tabernacle

10. Wenham, *Genesis 1–15*, 71.

11. Trible, *God and Rhetoric*, 105–15.

12. Barr, *The Garden of Eden*, 4.

as the place where God walked with God's people.[13] To be expelled from the Garden is to be expelled from the presence of God, to be cut off from the intimate relationship of regular communion with God as God "walks in the garden." That is the end of a relationship, or death. To the death of an intimate relationship with God, v. 22 adds the loss of the possibility of immortality through continued life in the Garden.

But that conclusion comes at the end of a crime and punishment narrative.

Hide and Seek, vv. 8–10.

Adam and the woman act like criminals. They run and hide (stated twice). God takes the initiative and comes looking and calling for them. Why did the man and the woman hide? The only answer given in the text is that "I was afraid, because I was naked." The couple is afraid of being naked before God. It is the couple's nakedness before God that represents something new and frightening. Adam and the woman are ashamed. There is no language or even suggestion of sin or guilt, consciousness of sin or consciousness of guilt in the text. The common Western interpretation of the narrative as "the Fall" with its accompanying theology of sin has been read back into the text. They have walked naked with God in the Garden before. They have had sex before and their nakedness was unitive ("one flesh," 2:24). Only one thing has changed because they have eaten from the forbidden fruit—they suddenly "see," a seeing that reveals something profoundly new about themselves, namely, that they are naked. They do not want to meet God naked. The text says nothing more, and we should not let Augustine, or Luther, or Freud, or anyone else tell us that there is more than the text says.

Interrogation and Defense, vv. 11–13

One question from God, "have you eaten from the tree of which I commanded you not to eat" (v. 11), establishes what has happened. Each confesses that "I ate" (vv. 12, 13), but only after blaming someone else: Adam blames the woman (v. 12), she blames the serpent (v. 13). Mistrust of God and disobedience of God leads to estrangement from each other.

---

13. Wenham, *Genesis 1–15*, 90.

The narrative sequence is important. In vv. 1–7 the sequence was serpent, woman, man. Here the sequence is man, woman. The serpent is mentioned, but is not interrogated by God. Humans have to answer for their choices and behavior. The assertion "you have done it" makes an action a crime against God, a "sin" although that word is not used. What constitutes a sin against God "is what people do in defiance of God and nothing else, not a consciousness of sin nor a bad conscience."[14]

The crime scene began with the serpent. There is no explanation of why the serpent tempted the woman. There is no interrogation of the serpent. The serpent is not forced to explain why it tempted the woman to eat the fruit. The intent of the author is not to offer an explanation of the origin of evil. The Bible does not offer an explanation of the origin of evil. Bonhoeffer was correct to observe that "the Bible does not seek to import information about the origin of evil but to witness to its character. . . . To pose the question about the origin of evil . . . is far from the mind of the biblical author."[15]

The Penultimate Punishment, vv. 14–19.

There is a remarkable difference between the ultimate punishment, expulsion from the garden, and the punishments enumerated in vv. 14–19. The expulsion from the garden is fixed in the structure of the narrative—God put man/woman in the garden, God drove them out of the garden. The punishments outlined in vv. 14–19 have no direct relationship with the offence; instead, they describe factually the state of existence of the serpent, the woman, and the man. Furthermore, the pronouncements of vv. 14–19 are in a different literary style from what precedes and what follows—the form is poetic. Some scholars believe that these verses were added by the editor(s) as a further elaboration. If that is true, the original and only punishment from God was the expulsion from the garden and alienation from God. Man/woman were expelled from the garden and were alienated from God.

The narrative sequence in vv. 14–19 follows the same pattern as in vv. 1–7: serpent, woman, man. The serpent only of the three parties is cursed via the use of an old curse formula, "cursed are you . . ." (v. 14). This curse as a direct address from God is found in the Old Testament only in 3:14 and 4:11. It represents an excommunication that separates the serpent

14. Westermann, *Genesis 1–11*, 255.
15. Bonhoeffer, *Creation and Fall*, 205.

The Story of Original Sin

from the rest of the animal kingdom because of its form and way of living. The curse explains the way in which the serpent moves and feeds itself.[16]

The "enmity" between the serpent and the woman in v. 15 defines a continual state of hostility, something that does not exist between humans and other animals, but only between humans and the serpent; each will literally seek to "grind" (*sup* in both phrases)—rather than "strike"—the head or heel of the other. Since the early church father Irenaeus (late second century CE) many commentators and preachers have understood v. 15 as a Christian prophecy about Christ and Mary. The "seed of the woman," Christ, was referred to one individual descendant who crushed the head of the serpent, whose seed was also an individual person, the devil or Satan.[17] Christian art and hymnology over many centuries has popularized this interpretation in the Western and Orthodox churches and cultures. However, this interpretation must be rejected for two reasons: 1) the word "seed" is collective, not singular; the NRSV and NIV translations "offspring" capture this collective understanding. The text is speaking of the line of descendants of the woman as well as of the serpent. 2) The word occurs in the context of the pronouncement of a curse. The form (form critically speaking) does not permit either a promise or prophecy as its primary or secondary meaning.[18] The woman is addressed in two clauses: v. 16a is a two parallel sentence structure which assigns pain in bearing children and in giving birth; v. 16b defines her relationship to her husband as desiring him and being subordinate to him. As Gerhard von Rad says, the woman's existence is described from two points of view: mother and wife.[19]

The address to the man is the longest and most detailed, and thus carries the most weight. Furthermore, it repeats the crime at the outset. It also uses a curse formula but in this case the curse is in the third person and is directed at the ground because of the man rather than directly at the man. The curse of the ground will be effective in the growth of thorns and thistles that will diminish the production of the crops and make the harvest difficult. The man will live and eat "by the sweat of your face" (v. 19a).

16. Trible, *God and Rhetoric*, 123–26.

17. The majority of church fathers did not follow Irenaeus, e.g., Basil of Caesarea, Gregory of Nazianzus, John Chrysostom in the East, Ambrose, Augustine, Jerome and Gregory the Great in the West.

18. See Hamilton, *Genesis 1–17*, 197–200, for a careful discussion of the language and issues; and Westermann, *Genesis 1–11*, 260.

19. Von Rad, *Genesis*, 96. See Trible, *God and Rhetoric*, 126–28, for an insightful analysis of the judgment on the woman.

V. 19b, "until you return to the ground for out of it you were taken," is a subordinate sentence to v. 19a. Death is not meant as a punishment; it is referred to as part of the natural order of things. Only with death will there be an end to hard work. V. 19c is a repetition of v. 19b, "you are dust, and to dust you shall return." The phrase is a fitting conclusion to the sentence of punishment in vv. 14–19. In their origin and destiny human beings belong to dust.[20]

Exegetes are divided over the question of whether death in this text was meant as a punishment for mistrusting and disobeying God. Some think death is a punishment. The majority argue that vv. 17–19 answer the question of why work is so burdensome. Man's return to the earth closes the life span that began with creation and liberates man from the toil of work. Still others see no difficulty in interpreting death both as a natural consequence of man's origin from the earth and as a punishment.[21]

THE CONCLUSION, VV. 20–24

Most commentators are agreed that the narrative of vv. 20–24 does not constitute a unity. The conclusion of the narrative is v. 24: God drove "the man" out of the garden." A number of other sentences have been added to the ultimate punishment narrative.

V. 20 presumes that the woman has given birth to a child. The man names his wife "Eve (= living) because she was the mother of all living." Some event must have occasioned the naming of the woman, and commentators presume it must have been the birth of a child. The blessing and the power of procreation has not been lost by the crime and punishment of disobedience to God. The man names the woman which is a chilling sign of domination even though he defines her as the bearer of life. The woman guarantees the future now in subordination to man.[22]

The verb "made" for "made garments of skin" in v. 21 is used only here and in the creation account. It refers to the unique creative activity of God. The last creative activity of God recorded in the Old Testament is an

20. The parallel expression "return to dust" is common in the OT—see Job 10:9; Ps 90:3; 146:3,4; also Sir 40:11.

21. See Westermann, *Genesis 1–11*, 266; Barr, *The Garden of Eden*, 4; Fretheim, "Fall Story," 152; Fretheim, *God and the World*, 76–77; Fretheim, "Genesis," 364; Goldingay, *Old Testament Theology*, 120; Hamilton, *Genesis*, 203; Trible, *God and Rhetoric*, 128–132; von Rad, *Genesis*, 95; Vawter, *On Genesis*, 85.

22. Trible, *God and Rhetoric*, 133–34.

act of covering and protecting God's creatures while putting them outside the garden, and at the same time distancing them from Godself.

V. 23 indicates that man expelled from the garden has a mission—it is to serve the earth. In 2.6 "there was no one to till the ground." Man's mission inside and outside the garden is to till the ground.

Vv. 22 and 24 belong together to form a single conclusion. So far in the narrative the reason for the expulsion from the garden is mistrust and disobedience. Vv. 22 and 24 add a second reason. Man and woman must be prevented from eating from the tree of life and living for ever. Chapter 3 has been concerned with one tree, "the tree of the knowledge of good and evil." It now returns to the "tree of life," mentioned before only in 2:9. "Knowledge of good and evil" and "eternal life" are two qualities that are peculiar to the Divine in the Old Testament, or the gods in the ancient world. Humans can and have acquired knowledge of good and evil. "Life forever" must be forbidden them. Therefore, the expulsion from the garden.

The punishment, vv. 14–24, indicate that every relationship in life and in culture is disrupted because of Adam and Eve's mistrust and disobedience—the relationship between an animal and God, between animals and humans, between man and woman, between humans and God. The beauty, harmony, and order of creation—the "it was good"—has been replaced by humiliation, domination, subordination, conflict, suffering, and struggle, and all of this with a fractured relationship with God.

SUMMARY

Eve and Adam are tempted by a creature of God, a serpent, to mistrust and disobey God by eating from the "tree of the knowledge of good and evil" which God had forbidden. Both the woman and Adam eat from the tree. They do not die immediately, but they are changed. They realize that they are naked, and they are afraid to meet God. The punishment for mistrusting and disobeying God is expulsion from the garden, which meant the loss of the intimate friendship with God that Adam and Eve enjoyed in the garden and the loss of the possibility of immortality. The mistrust and disobedience of Adam and Eve results in estrangement from God and exile from the Garden; exile means that "at homeness" is lost, fragmentation replaces unity and wholeness (*shalom*), death replaces the prospect of immortality.

Given all of the theological messages that have been overlaid on this text in the history of interpretation, it is important to note what is not present in the text—there is no association of the serpent with Satan or the demonic; Eve is not pictured as seducing Adam sexually or in any other way; the words "sin," "transgression," "rebellion," "guilt" in Hebrew or English are not used; there is no linkage between Adam and Eve's disobedience and sex. There is no hint that Adam's moral condition is fundamentally changed by his act of disobedience or that his essential human or genetic nature was essentially altered. The changes effected by the punishment for Adam and Eve's mistrust and disobedience are entirely physical, the pains and struggles of human life. There also is no hint in the following tragic story that the sin of Cain, his murder of his brother Abel, is a function of a morally defective nature that he inherited from Adam; "sin" used for the first time in the Bible in this story is defined as "lurking at the door," and Cain is advised by God that "you must master it" or "rule over it" (Gen. 4:7).

Equally important, and profoundly significant for the interpretive lens through which Christians have come to read the Genesis 3 narrative, the story does not speak of a "fall." The description of the disobedience of Adam and Eve as a "fall," notes Westermann, is an "inaccurate and deceptive" construal of what the text says.[23] The interpretation of Genesis 3 as a fall reflects a much later Christian understanding which has been read back into the text; the term "the fall" was first used with certainty to describe the sin of Adam by the Greek church father Methodius of Olympus, late third or early fourth century (d. 311), as a reaction to Origen's teaching of a prenatal fall in the transcendent world (see chapter 4) (the possible use of the word "fall" in 4 Ezra 7:118 is quite uncertain—see p. 29). In other words, a "fall" theology about the interpretation of Genesis 3 begins to develop about six to eight centuries after the probable writing of the original Genesis 3 story in a totally different setting and for a totally different purpose (many more centuries later if Genesis 3 is dated to the tenth century BCE). Why is it profoundly significant that this much later Christian and Greek "fall" construal is not stated or even suggested in the text? Because that means the story of salvation history, which is a fairly normative interpretive framework for a Christian reading the whole Bible does not begin with "the fall." Rather, it begins with broken relationships and exile, which is a very Jewish way of reading the text. And lest we forget, it was Jewish people who wrote this text originally for Jewish people, probably for Jewish people living in exile trying to understand the profound tragedy of the destruction of their country, the Temple, many of their fellow-countrymen (women/children), and their

---

23. Westermann, *Genesis 1–11*, 276.

exile in Babylon. The re-definition of the story of Genesis 3 as a "fall" represented a much later Hellenistic-Gentile re-interpretation of the text (but, that is getting ahead of our story).[24]

The sin in the Adam and Eve story is mistrust and disobedience of God that results in fractured relationships, in estrangement from God, from each other, from some animals (e.g., the snake), from creation (e.g., the land). Sin (though, let's remember the word is not used in the text of the story), in other words, is defined in *relational* terms, not ontological terms. What I was taught in church and college did not come from the Genesis story.

REFLECTIONS

The Genesis 3 narrative is one of the few biblical stories that is known all over the world even to this day. And, as with the re-telling of stories in all cultures, the story has changed significantly in the re-telling over time. The rest of this book will trace the changes that take place as the story was retold and re-interpreted in the texts that we have which re-tell and re-interpret the meaning Genesis 3 through the Christian theologian Augustine in the early fifth century CE.

One of the most surprising discoveries is that the story of Adam and Eve in Genesis 3 is not re-told again in the Hebrew Scriptures, the Christian Old Testament. The stories of the founding patriarchs—Abraham, Isaac, and Jacob—Moses, the liberator from slavery in Egypt and the covenant maker between God and Israel, and David, the first great king of the Israelite people, are retold often, but the story of Adam and Eve in Genesis is missing in the rest of the Old Testament. The first re-telling of the story narrated in Genesis 3 for which we have a record is found in the literature of Second Temple Judaism. For centuries the story of Adam and Eve's mistrust and disobedience of God seem not to have been important in the life and faith of the Israelite people.

24. It should be noted that some scholars take an even more radical stance and assert that neither the Genesis 3 story, nor the Old Testament as a whole, explicitly tie the sin and death of all human beings with Adam's sin. See, for example, Hamilton, *Genesis*, 213; and Neenan, "Doctrine of Original Sin," 58–59. Both scholars attribute the Adam sin/humanity sin/death linkage to Paul in Romans 5, and the Catholic Neenan cites the Council of Trent as support for his interpretation. Neenan is correct that the Council of Trent does not cite the Genesis 3 text, but bases its interpretation of original sin entirely on the Vulgate's and Augustine's mistranslation of Romans 5.12, "in whom all sinned." See Pelikan and Hotchkis, *Creeds and Confessions*, Vol. 2, 821–71, for the text of the Council of Trent.

2

The Story of Sin in Second Temple Judaism (200 BCE–200 CE)

THE BABYLONIAN EMPIRE DESTROYED the Israelite nation and the Temple in Jerusalem in 587 BCE, and took many Israelite people into exile within the Empire. There is general agreement that most of the writings that came to constitute the Hebrew Scriptures and the Christian Old Testament were completed during the exile, and that some form of an authoritative list of writings was being recognized by the middle second century BCE. At least Joshua ben Sirach knew of something like the tripartite division of the Hebrew Bible (Torah, Prophets, Writings) when he wrote the prologue for his grandfather's book of wisdom around 130 BCE.

The period between roughly the end of the fourth century BCE (the beginning of the exile) and the second century CE (even though the second temple was destroyed in 70 CE) is known as "Second Temple Judaism" (occasionally as "Middle Judaism"). The term indicates a time between early Judaism, or pre-exilic Judaism, and later Judaism, or the Judaism of the rabbis and beyond.

The Second Temple period was a time of great literary activity and theological reflection in Judaism.[1] I was asked in the 1980s to teach a six-week Wednesday evening course in a large Christian church in California, on the literature, theology, and culture of Second Temple Judaism. The

1. See Nickelsburg, *Jewish Literature*, for an introduction to this literature, and Nickelsburg, *Ancient Judaism*, for an introduction to the theology of this literature.

course was a requirement for a tour of the Middle East that the pastor was leading. I was to acquaint the fifty people enrolled with the larger historical, cultural, and theological context of the first century for understanding Jesus and the early church. To my chagrin I learned that the pastor had entitled the course "The Four Hundred Silent Years." I showed up for the first class with a stack of books documenting the literary activity of Second Temple Judaism—the Septuagint, the R. H. Charles translations of the apocryphal and pseudepigraphical writings, the Dead Sea Scrolls, the writings of Philo and Josephus, the writings of the early Jewish rabbis (the Mishnah). My opening line was that the years of Second Temple Judaism were anything but silent; they actually produced a much larger body of writings than was contained in the Christian Old and New Testaments. A good many of these writings, I noted in my introduction, were contained in the Catholic version of the Old Testament which Martin Luther unilaterally deleted from the Old Testament so that the Protestant Old Testament which they had was smaller than that of the early Christians and of their Catholic neighbors.

The Genesis 3 story of Adam and Eve, which we noted is missing in the rest of the Old Testament, is picked up in the literature of Second Temple Judaism around 200 BCE, and it is referenced in a variety of different kinds of literature.

WISDOM LITERATURE

The earliest re-telling of the Adam story in Second Temple Jewish Literature is found in a wisdom genre.

Sirach

The Adam story is re-told for the first time in *Sirach*, also known as the *Wisdom of Jesus the Son of Sirach* or *Ecclesiasticus*. It was written in Hebrew by Joshua Eleazar ben Sira, a professional scribe between 198–75 BCE, and translated into Greek by his grandson in 132 BCE.[2] The document consists of proverbs and meditations on wisdom. It is not found in the Jewish canon, but was included in the Christian canon of the Old Testament that the early Christians used (the Septuagint) and remained in the

---

2. Nickelsburg, *Jewish Literature*, 64; and Skehen and DiLella, *Wisdom of Ben Sira*, 8–10.

Christian canon until the Reformation. It is still in the Catholic Bible (e.g., the Jerusalem Bible) and some English Bibles (e.g., New English Bible, Oxford edition).

A significant reference to Adam occurs in a discourse on wisdom. Adam did not comprehend wisdom:

> The first man never managed to grasp her [wisdom] entirely,
>   nor has the most recent one fully comprehended her;
>   for her thoughts are wider than the sea,
>   and her designs more profound than the abyss.
>   (24:28, Jerusalem Bible)

A second reference is found in the context of a eulogy of Israel's ancestors, chapters 44–49. Adam is identified as the greatest of Israel's ancestors in 49:16: "above every living creature is Adam" (Jerusalem Bible).

The first man, Adam, lacked fullness of wisdom, but he was a glorious human being. He was the first Israelite, the patriarch of the Israelite people whose glory excelled all others. Temptation, disobedience, sin, expulsion from the Garden is not known in *Sirach*.[3]

Another important text in *Sirach* supports those interpreters of Genesis 3 who reject the view that death was a punishment for Adam and Eve's disobedience. In 17:1–7 *Sirach* states:

> The Lord fashioned man from the earth,
>   to consign him back to it.
> He gave them so many days' determined time,
>   he gave them authority over everything on earth,
> He clothed them with strength like his own,
>   and made them in his own image.
> He filled all living things with dread of man,
>   making him master over beasts and birds.
> He shaped for them a mouth and tongue, eyes and ears,
>   and gave them a heart to think with.
> He filled them with knowledge and understanding,
>   and revealed to them good and evil. (Jerusalem Bible)

In a clear reference to the Genesis 1–3 narrative, human mortality as well as the knowledge of good and evil are God's responsibility, not the result of Adam and Eve's disobedience in the Garden. Death is part of God's design for the first human couple, not a punishment for sin. This

---

3. For more on the theology this "Adam as the first Jew," see Scroggs, *Last Adam*; Levison, *Portraits of Adam*; Toews, *Romans*, 152; N. T. Wright, "Adam in Pauline Christology," 359–89; N. T. Wright, *Climax of the Covenant*, 18–40.

understanding is reinforced in 41:4 where *Sirach* asserts that death is "the Lord's decree for all flesh" and not a punishment for sin.[4]

But Sirach does contain a potential contradiction to this apparent vindication of Adam and Eve. In 25:24 he says, "sin began with a woman, and thanks to her we all must die." Since Augustine the unnamed female in this text has been identified as Eve in the Garden, and used as a proof-text for the doctrine of original sin.[5] But that identification has been challenged in recent times. Jack Levison outlines a careful argument that the text does not refer to Eve or to men generally but to a "wicked wife" and the husband of such wives, and thus should be translated as "from the (evil) wife is the beginning of sin," and because of her we (husbands) all die."[6] John Collins points out that the statement occurs in the middle of a series of diverse and negative sayings concerning the troubles women cause men (25:13–36), and accordingly says more about Sirach's mistrust of women than it does about his understanding of the Genesis 3 story.[7] Teresa Ellis' recent careful linguistic study concludes that the text cannot refer to Eve; she suggests that it refers to Hesiod's Pandora as the prototype for Ben Sira's figure of the Bad Wife as a contrast for the biblical Valorous Wife in order to undermine Hellenistic presumptions of cultural superiority.[8]

The statement that God "filled them with knowledge and understanding and revealed to them good and evil" in 17:6–7 is remarkable compared to the explicit assertion in Genesis that God forbade Adam and

4. See Collins, "Before the Fall," 296–97; see also Kugel, *Traditions*, 96–97, 127 for a tradition in Second Temple Judaism which understands death either as part of God's design for human beings or interprets the "you shall die" statement in Genesis 3 to mean that Adam and Eve were created to be immortal "if they obeyed the rules," but that they would lose their immortality and become subject to death after a normal life (930 years in the case of Adam) if they disobeyed God. Kugel himself believes that *Sirach* in 17:1–2 may be implying that "Adam had always been intended for mortality, his very creation from the earth embodying his intended end after the 'numbered days and time' allotted to him had been exhausted" (ibid., 127).

5. See Ellis, "Is Eve the Woman?" 723.

6. See Levison, "Is Eve to Blame?" 617–23. Skehan and DiLella, *Wisdom of Ben Sira*, 349, find Levison's argument unpersuasive. See also Kugel, *Traditions*, 100–102, for other Second Temple Jewish writers who place the blame for human sinfulness on Eve or women. Sirach 2.24 makes the envy of the devil, rather than humans responsible for the entry of death into the world. See also Hogan, "The Exegetical Background of the 'Ambiguity of Death,'" 18–19.

7. See Collins, "Before the Fall," 298. Stokes, "The Origin of Sin in the Scrolls," 56, agrees with Collins' understanding. See Sirach 42:12–14 for another series of statements that reflect his negative view of women.

8. See Ellis, "Is Eve the 'Woman'?" 723–42.

Eve to eat from the tree of knowledge of good and evil on pain of death. Sirach clearly had a different understanding of the Genesis text. But it should be noted that there are several texts from the Dead Sea Scrolls that also claim that God endowed Adam with wisdom and knowledge at the time of creation. 4Q504 (fragment 8) says that when God made Adam in his image he blew into his nostril the breath of life, and intelligence and knowledge.[9] 4Q303, a meditation on creation, speaks of "the knowledge of good and evil" before the creation of Eve. The knowledge of good and evil in one tradition of interpretation was not prohibited to humans and was not linked to the disobedience of God.

Sirach continues in 17:8–12 by saying that God

> Set knowledge before them,
>> he endowed them with the law of life.
> He established an eternal covenant with them,
>> and revealed his judgments to them.
> Their eyes saw his glorious majesty,
>> and their ears hear the glory of his voice.
> He said to them, "Beware of all wrongdoing";
>> he gave each a commandment concerning his neighbor.
> (Jerusalem Bible)

God made a covenant with Adam and gave him commandments right from the beginning. Sirach, says Collins, "seems to collapse the time difference between Genesis and Deuteronomy."[10]

In addition, it should be noted that Sirach had a very high theology of human free will and of the human ability to keep the Torah:

> Do not say, "The Lord was responsible for my sinning,"
>> For he is never the cause of what he hates.
> Do not say, "It was he who led me astray,"
>> For he has no use for a sinner.
> The Lord hates all that is foul,
>> and no one who fears him will love it either.
> He himself made man in the beginning,
>> and then left him free to make his own decision.
> If you wish, you can keep the commandments,
>> to behave faithfully is within your power.
> He has set fire and water before you;
>> put out your hand to whichever you prefer.

9. See Collins, "Before the Fall," 299–300; and Chazon, "The Creation and Fall of Adam," 15.

10. Collins, "Before the Fall," 299.

> Man has life and death before him;
>> whichever a man likes better will be given him.
> For vast is the wisdom of the Lord;
>> he is almighty and all-seeing.
> His eyes are on those who fear him,
>> he notes every action of man.
> He never commanded anyone to be godless,
>> he has given no one permission to sin.
> (15:11–20, Jerusalem Bible)

Sirach is clear that humans were created with free choice and the capacity to obey the Torah; they are responsible to choose between sin and obedience of God's law.[11] There is no such thing as "original sin," biological or social, which predisposes people to disobey God and choose sin.

The earliest reading of the Genesis 3 story presents a quite remarkable interpretation. Adam is a hero; he is the model Israelite. There is no fateful event that changed the circumstances of human life let alone human nature. Neither sin nor death can be blamed on the disobedience of Adam (or Eve). Death is decreed by God for all flesh, and sin is the responsibility of every human being.

Wisdom of Solomon (also called the Book of Wisdom)

Composed in Egypt in the early decades of the Common Era, probably during the reign of the Roman Emperor Caligula (37–41 CE), the Wisdom of Solomon is an apologetic to Jews who had abandoned the law for Greek culture.[12] It was an exhortation to pursue wisdom and thereby the righteous life which issues in immortality. The Wisdom of Solomon, like Sirach, was in the canon of the Old Testament of the early Christians and remained in the Christian canon until the Reformation, and remains in the Catholic Bible.

Adam is referenced in chapter 10 as the first of seven heroes whom wisdom saved. He is contrasted with his son Cain.

> The father of the world, the first being to be fashioned,
> created alone, he had her [wisdom] for his protector
> and she delivered him from his fault;
> she gave him the strength to subjugate all things.

---

11. See Collins, "Before the Fall," 299; and Kugel, *Traditions*, 130–32, for other Second Temple Jewish affirmations of human free will.

12. See Nickelsburg, *Jewish Literature*, 184.

But when a sinner in his wrath deserted her,
he perished in his fratricidal fury. (10:1–2, Jerusalem Bible)

Adam is the father of the world who rules the world, who "subjugates all things" because of his reliance on wisdom. Furthermore, Adam was preserved from sinning by means of wisdom. The verb *disphulassein* in v. 1 means "protected" elsewhere in Wisdom of Solomon. Wisdom preserved Adam from the time of creation so that he did not transgress later in life.

Adam is the model of the just and godly person, v. 1. Cain is the type of godless person, v. 2. He is responsible for evil in the world; he is the cause of the flood. Death entered the world because of Cain.

Adam is the Israelite hero. He is the first Israelite whom wisdom saved from transgression and whom wisdom empowered to rule the world. Adam is the model that contemporary Jews should emulate.[13]

Interpretive Pause

The two wisdom writings that re-tell the Adam story in Second Temple Judaism picture him as a heroic Israelite figure. Adam is the patriarch of the Jewish people, a man of great wisdom who is the image of the humanity God intended in creation. This form of Adam theology advanced a claim about the place of Israel in the purposes of God. Israel is God's true humanity who fulfill's God's destiny by obeying the Torah. This Adam theology was transposed into nationalist ideology during the Maccabean period, 165–63 BCE, and the anti-Roman reaction that resulted in the Jewish-Roman War of 66–70 CE and the destruction of the Temple in 70 CE.

There is no theology of sin, let alone any notion of a "fall" or of "original sin" in this literature. Adam is the model for the Jewish people, not the problem for humanity. Mortality, Sirach suggests, was part of God's plan from the beginning, not a function of Adam's sin.

It is important to note that many scholars think that Paul was familiar with the second of these writings, the Wisdom of Solomon, especially in his writing of Romans 1. If that is the case, the writer of Wisdom and Paul understand the role of Adam in history very differently.

13. Levison, *Portraits of Adam*, 59–62.

HISTORICAL WRITINGS

Another body of Second Temple literature that re-tells the Adam story is best described as history or re-written biblical history.

The Book of Jubilees

The book, generally dated between 175–100 BCE, re-tells the biblical narrative of Genesis 1 through Exodus 12 with extensive elaboration. It was written in Hebrew and then translated into Greek. Fragments of Hebrew manuscripts have been found among the Dead Sea Scrolls. The critical theme in Jubilees is the importance of obeying the law as the antidote to the disintegrating effects of Hellenism. Adam is portrayed as the first of the patriarchs. He and the other patriarchs are depicted as observing the Torah even before it was given.[14]

The story of Genesis 3 is retold in Jubilees 3:15–35 as follows:

> And during the first week of the first jubilee Adam and his wife had been in the garden of Eden for seven years tilling and guarding it. . . . [W]e [angels] were teaching him to do everything which was appropriate for tilling. And he was naked, but he neither knew it nor was he ashamed. . . . At the end of seven years which he completed here, seven years exactly, in the second month on the seventeenth day, the serpent came and drew near to the woman . . . and she ate. And she first covered her shame with a fig leave, and then she gave it to Adam and he ate and his eyes were opened and he saw that he was naked. And he took a fig leaf and sewed it and made an apron for himself. And he covered his shame.
>
> And to Adam he [God] said, "Because you listened to the voice of your wife and you ate from that tree from which I commanded you that you should not eat, the land shall be cursed because of you . . ."
>
> And he made them garments of skin and he dressed them and sent them from the garden of Eden. And on that day when Adam went out from the garden of Eden, he offered a sweet-smelling sacrifice—franchincense, galbanum, stacte, and spices—in the morning with the rising of the sun from the day he covered his shame. On that day the mouth of all the beasts and cattle and birds and whatever walked or moved was stopped from speaking because all of them used to speak with one another with

14. Nickelsburg, *Jewish Literature*, 73–74; Wintermute, "Jubilees," 35–44.

one speech and one language. And he sent from the garden of Eden all of the flesh which was in the garden of Eden and all of the flesh was scattered, each according to its kind and each one according to its family, and into the place which was created for them. But from all the beasts and the cattle he granted to Adam alone that he might cover his shame. Therefore, it is commanded in the heavenly tablets to all who will know the judgment of the Law that they should cover their shame and they should not be uncovered as the gentiles are uncovered.

And on the first of the fourth month Adam and his wife went out from the garden of Eden and dwelt in the land of Elda, in the land of their creation. And Adam named his wife Eve. They had no son until the first jubilee but after this he knew her. And he tilled the land as he had been taught in the garden of Eden.[15]

Adam and Eve disobey God's command after seven years of celibate life together in the Garden. Adam obediently offered sacrifices as he and Eve left the Garden; that is, Adam acted like a priest on the way out of the Garden. The effect of Adam and Eve's eating from the forbidden tree was not universal sin but the loss of speech of all animals and birds so that they could no longer communicate with one another as they used to in "one speech and one language." The moral lesson of the clothing of Adam and Eve was that nakedness as practiced among the pagans was prohibited among God's people. Adam and Eve consummated the marriage sexually after leaving the Garden following seven years of living together in Edenic bliss, and a son was born.

Jewish Antiquities

The *Antiquities* is a long explanation and apology for Judaism to the Romans written by Josephus (37–100 CE), a first century Jewish warrior/historian/apologist, following the destruction of Jerusalem. Josephus offers an interpretation of Genesis 3 in 1:40–51. The serpent tempted Adam and Eve because he was jealous of Adam's good standing with God. He knew God's retributive scheme: obedience led to blessing, disobedience would lead to calamity. What Adam and Eve gained by eating the fruit of the forbidden tree was intelligence, which was a good thing. The increased intelligence represented a positive change. The problem was that a good was attained without God. The lesson of the Adam and Eve story

---

15. Translation by Wintermute, Charlesworth, *OTP*, vol. 1, 59–60.

was that wisdom attained without God leads to irretrievable disaster. The other lesson of the Adam and Eve story was that Adam was punished because he listened to the lesser counsel of a woman. Female counsel must not be heeded. Adam and Eve did not lose immortality, but the good life as defined in Greek terms.[16]

DEAD SEA SCROLLS

One of the most important manuscript discoveries of the twentieth century were the Dead Sea Scrolls in the caves above the Dead Sea in 1948 and years following; approximately 800 scrolls or fragments of scrolls were found.[17] The Scrolls offer two explanations of sin from different texts in Genesis. The first explanation, and the more common one in the centuries before the common era, was based on the Genesis 6 story of the "sexual relations" between "the sons of God" and "the daughters of men." This union, it was believed, produced "super-human" beings who later were interpreted as "evil spirits" who were responsible for sin in the world.[18]

The second explanation provides a commentary on the creation story in Genesis 1 and a very different interpretation of responsibility for sin. *The Community Rule* (1QS), discovered in Cave 1, and considered by many scholars to be the oldest document of the Qumran sect, was a kind of instructional manual intended for teachers of the community inhabiting what we today call the Qumran community. Chapter 3:12f is called "The Treatise on the Two Spirits" because of the way it contrasts two spirits in the world. The Treatise begins with a declaration of the absolute sovereignty of God:

> From the God of Knowledge comes all that is and shall be.
> Before ever they existed He established their whole design, and
> when, as ordained for them, they come into being, it is in accord
> with His glorious design that they accomplish their task without

---

16. Levison, *Portraits of Adam*, 99–108.

17. See Vanderkam, *The Dead Sea Scrolls*, for an accessible introduction to the Dead Sea Scrolls.

18. See "The Book of Watchers" in 1 Enoch 1–36, especially 6–11; Jubilees 4:22, 5:1–10, 7:21; Testament of Reuben 5; Testament of Naphtali 3:5; Damascus Document 2:18–21; and Nickelsburg, *Ancient Judaism*, 63–64; Stokes, "The Origin of Sin in the Scrolls," 57–63; Collins, "Before the Fall," 301–5; Collins, "The Origin of Evil in Apocalyptic Literature and the Scrolls," 287–99; and Boccaccini, *Beyond the Essene Hypothesis*.

change. The law of all things are in His hands and He provides them with all their needs.[19]

The text then goes on with a clear reference to the Genesis 1:1—2:4a creation narrative:

> He has created man to govern the world, and has appointed for him two spirits in which to walk until the time of His visitation: the spirits of truth and injustice. Those born of truth spring from a fountain of light, but those born of injustice spring from a source of darkness. All the children of righteousness are ruled by a Prince of Light and walk in the ways of light, but all the children of injustice are ruled by the Angel of Darkness and walk in the ways of darkness. The Angel of Darkness leads all the children of righteousness astray, and until his end, all their sin . . . and all their unlawful deeds are caused by his dominion in accordance with the mysteries of God. . . .
>
> But the God of Israel and His Angel of Truth will succour all the sons of light. For it is He who created the spirits of Light and Darkness and founded every action upon them and established every deed [upon] their [ways] . . .[20]

The text is clear—God created two spirits for humans, one of truth and light and the other of injustice and darkness. Both spirits have "superhuman" qualities or powers which play out in the conflict between good and evil. Where did the spirit of evil, the spirit of injustice and darkness, come from? God created it. Humans have qualities or virtues from both spirits because God gave both spirits to them (see 1QS 4:3–11). The problem of sin in *The Community Rule* is not the "marriage" of "the sons of God" and "the daughters of men" in Genesis 6, or the disobedience of Adam and Eve in Genesis 3, but God's creation of two spirits in Genesis 1. As John Collins so clearly points out, a very different ideology is assumed here, a "dualism was instituted by God as part of creation itself."[21] We are now a long way from Genesis 3, or Sirach, or the Wisdom of Solomon, but we are in the diversity of Second Temple Judaism and the approximate time-frame of the Apostle Paul.

---

19. *1QS 3.21*, Vermes, *Dead Sea Scrolls*, 101.

20. *1QS 3.19–25*, Ibid., 101–2.

21. Collins, "The Origin of Evil," 293; see also Levison, "The Two Spirits in Qumran Theology," 169–204, on the possible origins of the dualism. In addition, see Stuckenbruck, "The Interiorization of Dualism within the Human Being in Second Temple Judaism," 145–68; and Davidson, *Angels at Qumran*, 297.

Finally, several other themes in the Scrolls contain ideas that were present in other Second Temple Jewish literature. The notion from Sirach 17 that Adam was created with "understanding, knowledge" is stated explicitly in 4Q504.[22] Understanding and knowledge in Sirach and some of the Scrolls is a gift of creation prior to Adam's disobedience. Secondly, the same text, 4Q504, also states that Adam was mortal prior to his disobedience: "Thou didst enjoin him not to stray . . .he is flesh and to dust he will return . . ." (Vermes, 367). Third, the idea of Adam as the hero and model for the Jewish people is asserted twice in the Scrolls, *The Community Rule* 4:23 and the *Damascus Document* 3:20. In the first those who follow the "Spirit of Truth" will receive "the glory of Adam," while in the second the faithful remnant (the members of the community) will receive "the glory of Adam." Adam is the goal, not the problem.[23]

APOCALYPTIC WRITINGS

A fourth body of Second Temple writings retell the Adam and Eve story in very different terms than the first three. These writings are written following the destruction of Jerusalem and the Temple in 70 CE at the conclusion of the Jewish-Roman War of 66–70 CE. The trauma of these events led to an intense theological struggle to understand and explain why God permitted this catastrophic tragedy to occur. How could the God who elected Israel and who chose to be present with God's people in the Holy City, especially in the Temple, permit the destruction of the City and the Temple? 4 Ezra and 2 Baruch invoke the story of Adam and Eve to help explain the tragedy of 70 CE.

Fourth Ezra (also called Second Esdras)

Written at the end of the first century CE (ca. 100 CE), or thirty years after the destruction of the Temple, *4 Ezra* is a pseudonymous work organized around a series of dialogues between Ezra, the questioner, and Uriel, an angelic responder.[24] The dialogues present two pictures of Adam, those

22. 4Q504, Words of the Heavenly Lights" (trans. Vermes, 367). See also 4Q303, Meditation on Creation A, and 4Q305, Meditation on Creation B; and Chazon, "The Creation and Fall of Adam," 15, 19.

23. See Vermes, *Dead Sea Scrolls*, 103 and 129; and Vermes, "Genesis 1–3 in Post-Biblical Hebrew and Aramaic Literature," 223.

24. Nickelsburg, *Jewish Literature*, 297–98; Metzger, "Fourth Book of Ezra," 520;

of Ezra and those of Uriel; they are similar in that they address common issues, but different due to divergent solutions to the issues by Ezra, the human, and Uriel, the angelic agent.

Chapter 3:4–27 is a prayer of Ezra situated in Babylon seeking to understand the destruction of Jerusalem:

> vv. 4–11—O sovereign Lord, did you not speak at the begin-ning when you formed the earth—and that without help—and commanded the dust and it gave you Adam, a lifeless body? Yet he was the workmanship of your hands, and you breathed into him the breath of life, and he was made alive in your pres-ence. And you led him into the garden which your right hand had planted before the earth appeared. And you laid upon him one commandment of yours; but he transgressed it, and imme-diately you appointed death for him and for his descendants. From him there sprang nations and tribes, peoples and clans, without number. And every nation walked after its own will and did ungodly things before you and scorned you, and you did not hinder them. But again, in its time you brought the flood upon the inhabitants of the world and destroyed them. And the same fate befell them. As death came upon Adam, so the flood upon them. But you left one of them, Noah with his household . . .

vv. 12–19 is a narrative of the patriarchs.

> vv. 20–27—Yet you did not take away from them their evil heart, so that your Law might bring forth fruit in him. For the first Adam, burdened with an evil heart, transgressed and was overcome, as were also all who were descended from him. Thus the disease became permanent; the law was in the people's heart along with the evil root, but what was good departed, and the evil remained. So the times passed and the years were com-pleted, and you raised up for yourself a servant, named David. And you commanded him to build a city for your name . . . but the inhabitants of the city transgressed, in everything doing as Adam and all his descendants had done, for they also had the evil heart. So you delivered the city into the hands of your enemies.[25]

God appointed death for Adam and his descendants because of Adam's transgression. Death is hereditary. But this straightforward state-ment is complicated by what follows. All the nations sinned because God

---

Stone, *Fourth Ezra*, 9–10.

25. Translation by Metzger, Charlesworth, *OTP*, vol. 1, 528–29.

did not prevent them from sinning ("you did not hinder them"), and they suffered the punishment of the flood. So, death became a possibility with Adam and a reality because all sinned.

In addition, God created Adam with a weakness, with an evil heart. God gave Adam a commandment which he did not keep. The "disease" of the evil heart became a permanent condition of humanity. The Torah was given to overcome the evil heart, but it was not able. Why was the Holy City and the Temple destroyed? Because the inhabitants of the City transgressed the Torah just as Adam and his descendants had done.

Fourth Ezra is quite clear that Adam was "burdened with an evil heart" and that it became permanent in his offspring (3:22, 25–26; cf. 7:63–72), but the writer is careful to avoid directly attributing the creation of this evil inclination to God (see also 4:30 which uses a different image, seed and sowing: "For a grain of evil seed was sown in Adam's heart from the beginning"). In 3:20 God is charged for not removing the evil heart at the time of the giving of the Torah so that the Torah would be effective in leading to righteousness. Rabbinic sources, which are later than *4 Ezra*, are specific about the origin of the evil heart. God created the evil inclination, but God also gave humans the ability to overcome it through free will and the obedience of the Torah.[26]

The inheritance of the evil inclination in Adam's descendants stands in tension with the idea of free will in *4 Ezra*. The writer argues strongly and repeatedly for free will (7:19–24, 116–26; 8:56–62; 14:34; cf also 2 Apoc Bar 15:6; 54:21; 84; 85:7), and in a series of passages humankind is described as struggling to overcome the evil inclination and achieve righteousness (7:18, 92).[27]

As John R. Levison says, "Ezra draws only a correspondence, not a causal connection between the death of Adam and the sinful nations."[28] As Adam sinned, so did his descendants in general and Israel in particular.

Chapter 7:116–26 is a lament by Ezra over the fate of the mass of humanity:

26. See Urbach, *The Sages*, 420–36, 471–83 for the rabbinic discussion of sin and the two inclinations. As Urbach points out, in rabbinic Judaism "all men die on account of their sins," (ibid., 427), and there is no "idea of inherited sin" in rabbinic Judaism.

27. See Stone, *Fourth Ezra*, 63–73. For the rabbinic debate about the relationship of providence to free will, see Urbach, *The Sages*, 255–85. For a different view of free will in one part of Hellenistic Judaism, see Winston, "Philo's Doctrine of Free Will," 181–95.

28. Levison, *Portraits of Adam*, 116.

> This is my first and last word: it would have been better if the earth had not produced Adam, or else, when it had produced him, had restrained him from sinning. For what good is it to all that they live in sorrow now and expect punishment after death? O Adam, what have you done? For though it was you who sinned, *the fall*[29] was not yours alone, but ours also who are your descendants. For what good is it to us, if an eternal age has been promised to us, but we have done deeds that bring death? And what good is it that an everlasting hope has been promised us, but we have miserably failed. . . . For while we lived and committed iniquity we did not consider what we should suffer after death.[30]

In this text the earth created Adam, as also in 4:40, in contrast to 3:4 where God commanded the dust to form humanity. The earth should have taught Adam not to sin, whereas in 3:8 God was charged for not preventing humans from sinning. Two actions here that are attributed to earth–creation of humankind and the prevention of humans sinning–were more naturally attributed to God in chapter 3.

V. 118 is a restatement of 3:20–22, which spoke of the sin of Adam affecting all of his descendants. The result, Ezra goes on to lament, is a terrible fate for humanity. The promise of a reward is useless because all will be punished for sin anyway.

The angel's response to Ezra's lament is given in 7:127–31. It emphasizes free will and human responsibility. The angel rejects the idea of "original sin," which Ezra seems to have implied, and asserts that humankind has been given freedom of action and the consequent possibility of reward and punishment (vv. 127–28). You knew this, the angel says, since scripture states this explicitly (vv. 129–30).

---

29. The word translated *"the fall"* (the italics are mine) is based on the Latin translation, *casus*. The Latin text on which the translation is based was the Codex Sangermanensis, dated 822 CE, which was a translation from the Greek translation of the Hebrew text. Both original Hebrew text and the Greek translation have been lost. The other translations from the Greek text use broader terms in place of the word *casus*, e.g., "evil" (Syriac and Ethiopic), "sentence" or "damage" (Aramaic), "misfortune" or "suffering" (Armenian). As far as can be determined the first time the word "fall" is used to describe the disobedience of Adam in the Garden is Methodius of Olympus in the late fourth century CE. But the word used by Methodius and the later Latin Fathers was *lapsus* not the *casus* of *IV Ezra*. The Latin translation of the 9th century would appear to reflect the dominant understanding which "fall" language achieved in the Western Church. See Metzger, "Fourth Ezra," 518–20; Stone, *Fourth Ezra*, 258–59; Thompson, *Responsibility for Evil*, 325, for the textual tradition of 4 Ezra.

30. Metzger, Charlesworth, *OTP*, vol. 1, 541.

The dialogue in *4 Ezra* is clear that Adam's transgression in the Garden had consequences for his descendants. Adam was punished with death and that consequence was passed on to his descendants. A second result of Adam's sin was that life on earth became toilsome and difficult (see 7:12). Some in the circle of *4 Ezra* believed that Adam was created with an evil inclination that God should have removed at the time of the giving of the Torah, but the angel countered that humans had free will to obey the Torah rather than the evil heart.

The dialogues in *4 Ezra* indicate that there was a debate in Judaism at the end of the first century/beginning of the second century CE concerning hereditary sinfulness and individual responsibility. Ezra and Uriel are agreed that Adam was the first sinner, and that his transgression introduced death into the world. If Ezra reflects a disposition of some to say that sin is inevitable because of heredity from Adam, Uriel rejects it in favor of full human responsibility. In the end Ezra also agrees with this interpretation. Ezra cries in 7:118, "O Adam, what have you done? For though it was you who sinned, the 'misfortune' was not yours alone, but ours also who are your descendants."

Second Baruch

Second Baruch, like *4 Ezra,* was written at the end of the first century or early second century CE, also in an attempt to understand the catastrophe of 70 CE.[31] It contains seven episodes of dialogues between a human seer and a heavenly angel. The pessimism of *4 Ezra* is more profound than in *2 Baruch* because the latter believes that it is possible for humans to obey the Law, as Moses did.

> 17:1—18:2: With the Most High no account is taken of much time and of few years. For what did it profit Adam that he lived nine hundred and thirty years and transgressed that which he was commanded? Therefore, the multitude of time that he lived did not profit him, but it brought death and cut off the years of those who were born from him. Or what did it harm Moses that he lived only one hundred and twenty years and, because he subjected himself to him who created him, he brought the Law to the descendants of Jacob and he lighted a lamp to the generation of Israel?

31. See Nickelsburg, *Jewish Literature,* 81, 287; Klijn, "2 (Syriac Apocalypse of) Baruch)," 617.

And I answered and said: He who lighted took from the light, and there are few who imitated him. But many whom he illuminated took from the darkness of Adam and did not rejoice in the light of the lamp.[32]

Adam chose to disobey a commandment given him by God. Moses in contrast chose to submit to God. Historically Adam is the father of all. Adam's disobedience brought death to all, including those who obeyed the law. Theologically he is the father of the unrighteous, of those who chose to imitate him rather than Moses.

> 48:40: For each of the inhabitants of the earth knew when he acted unrighteously.

> 48:42–47: O Adam, what did you do to all who were born after you? And what will be said of the first Eve who obeyed the serpent, so that this whole multitude is going to corruption? And countless are those whom the fire devours. . . .

> You, O Lord, my Lord, you know that which is your creation, for you commanded the dust one day to produce Adam, and you knew the number of those who were born from him and how they sinned before you, those who existed and who did not recognize you as their Creator. And concerning all those, their end will put them to shame, and your Law which they transgressed will repay them on your day.[33]

Disobedience or unrighteous behavior is an act of free choice. The wicked are responsible for their sins, and the law "which they transgressed will repay them." That is, Adam and Eve are not responsible for the sin of their posterity.

The reference to Eve is important; it indicates that the author is aware of a tradition that implicates her in the transgression in the Garden.

> 54:15–19: For, although Adam sinned first and has brought death upon all who were not in his own time, yet each of them who has been born from him has prepared for himself the coming torment. . . . Adam is, therefore not the cause, except only for himself, but each of us has become our own Adam.[34]

---

32. Translated by Klijn, Charlesworth, *OTP*, vol. 1, 627.

33. Ibid., 637.

34. Ibid., 640.

Adam as the author of death recalls chapter 17:2–3. But each person born from him is accountable for his or her own judgment. Thus Adam is responsible only for himself, and everyone else "has become our own Adam."

The key concept for 2 *Baruch* is imitation. Adam did not cause his descendants to sin. Rather they chose to sin by imitating his disobedience. Adam, says Levison, is the paradigmatic figure for freedom of choice and responsibility.[35] Why is Adam made the model for individual responsibility? Levison suggests the author is responding to a view in which hereditary sinfulness was attributed to Adam's transgression.[36]

Summary

It seems clear from the two apocalyptic writers at the end of the first and beginning of the second century CE that the notion of the hereditary transmission of sin from Adam was being advocated by some people. Both *4 Ezra* and *2 Baruch* reject it in favor of individual responsibility for sin, *4 Ezra* less equivocally than *2 Baruch*. *Fourth Ezra* raises the question while the angel rejects it (7:127–31). In *2 Baruch* the question (48:42) is rebutted immediately for a theology of individual responsibility.

Life of Adam and Eve

A very different narrative was written in Hebrew somewhere between 100–200 CE, and then translated into Greek and Latin between then and 400 CE (it was also translated into Armenian, Gregorian, and Slavonic). The story is currently available in two recensions, *The Life of Adam and Eve* and *The Apocalypse of Moses*. The two accounts overlap considerably and are printed in parallel columns in Charlesworth *Old Testament Pseudepigrapha*.[37] The story currently tends to be studied most in its Greek translation as the "Greek Life of Adam and Eve" (*GLAE*). But it must be supplemented by the parallel narrative of *The Apocalypse of Moses* (*Apoc*

---

35. Levison, *Portrait of Adam*, 130.

36. Ibid., 138.

37. See the Johnson translation in Charlesworth, *OTP*, vol. 2, 249–95. On the translation of the *Life of Adam and Eve* see also Arbel, Cousland, and Neufeld, "And So They Went Out," xv, 3. Nickelsburg, *Jewish Literature*, 253–57, provides some background on the two documents. For more background on *The Life of Adam and Eve* see Stone, *Literature of Adam and Eve*, and de Jonge and Tromp, *The Life of Adam and Eve*.

Mos). GLAE is an edited work that seems to have circulated orally prior to being compiled in written form. The person responsible for sin in this narrative is Eve. But the story juxtaposes a number of overlapping and, at times, conflicting traditions about a blameworthy Eve as well as alternative traditions about a praiseworthy Eve.

The dominant scenes associate Eve with acts of wrongdoing. In these scenes Eve is characterized as a wicked figure who transgressed God's ways, as Adam's deceitful wife, and as an errant woman who was attracted to the sins of the flesh.

> 3:1: And Eve said to Adam, "My Lord, would you kill me? O that I would die! Then perhaps the Lord God will bring you again into Paradise, for it is because of me that the Lord God is angry with you."[38]

> 5:2: Eve to Adam: "I have brought toil and tribulation on you."[39]

A statement by Satan in chapter 16.3 explains why he approached and tempted Eve: "Because Satan was expelled from the heaven because he did not worship Adam as the image of God, 'I assailed your wife and made you to be expelled through her from the joys of your bliss, as I have been expelled from my glory.'"[40]

In chapters 10–11 the devil deceives Eve again by interrupting her repentance in the Jordan river; he persuades her that God has heard her cry for repentance and that she should come out of the river and eat food that has been prepared. When Adam sees her, he cries out that she has been deceived a second time: "O wicked woman! What have you done to us. You have deprived me of the glory of God."[41]

A little later God explains to Adam why he is being judged: "God said to me, 'Behold, you shall die, because you have disregarded the command of God, since you have listened rather to the voice of your wife, whom I gave into your power, that you might keep her in your will. But you listened to her and disregarded my words.'"[42]

Another series of narratives explain how Satan led Eve astray and the consequences for Adam:

38. Johnson, Charlesworth, *OTP*, vol. 2, 258.
39. Ibid., 258.
40. Ibid., 262.
41. Johnson, *Apoc Mos*, 21.6, Charlesworth, *OTP*, vol. 2, 281.
42. Johnson, *GLAE*, 26.2, Charlesworth, *OTP*, vol. 2, 268.

33:1–2: God created Adam and Eve and placed them in Paradise and told them not to eat of the tree of the knowledge of good and evil.

The Lord appointed two angels to guard us. The hour came when the angels ascended to worship in the presence of God. Immediately the adversary, the devil, found opportunity while the angels were away and deceived your mother, so that she ate of the illicit and forbidden tree. And she ate and gave to me.[43]

34:1–3: And immediately the Lord God was angry with us and the Lord said to me, "Because you have forsaken the command-ment and have not kept my word which I set before you, behold, I will bring upon your body seventy plagues; you shall be racked with various pains. . . . [T]he Lord sent all these to me and to all our generations."[44]

35:1–3: Adam said this to all his sons while he was seized with great pains, and he cried out with a loud voice saying, "Why should I suffer misery and endure such agony?" And when she saw him weeping, Eve herself began to weep, saying, "O Lord, my God, transfer his pain to me, since it is I who sinned." And Eve said to Adam, "My Lord, give me a portion of your pain, for this guilt has come to you for me."[45]

Eve's role as transgressor of God's command is amplified in several scenes that associate her with God's ultimate opponent, the Devil. *The Apocalypse of Moses* includes a description of the Devil beseeching Eve: "Fear not, only be my vessel and I will speak through your mouth words to deceive them" (16.5). And *Apoc Mos* presents the Devil turning Eve into his vessel and spokesperson, as she is made to attest, "For when he came, I opened my mouth and the Devil was speaking . . ." (21.3).

In Genesis 3 Eve's sin is not associated with illicit sexuality or sexual temptation. But *Apoc Mos* presents the transgression in the Garden as sexual in nature. *The Apocalypse of Moses* 19:3 pictures the serpent placing the "poison of wickedness" in the fruit that Eve ate, and identifies this poison as desire—*epithumia*—which is ultimately declared as the origin of every sin: "he came and entered and placed upon the fruit the poison of his wickedness—which is (the sense of) desire, for it is the beginning

---

43. Ibid., 272.

44. Ibid.

45. Ibid.

of every sin—and he bent the branch on the earth and I took of the fruit and ate."[46]

Eve not only ingests the Devil's/serpent's poison of wickedness, but also becomes responsible for introducing unlawful desire into the world. This carnal aspect of Eve's sin is further insinuated in God's accusing sentence in *Apoc Mos* 25.3: "But you shall confess and say: 'Lord, Lord, save me, and I will turn no more to the sin of the flesh.' But even another time you shall so turn."[47]

But *GLAE* offers an alternative, very different conceptualization of Eve. Several scenes characterize her as an ethical and moral figure, as Adam's devoted and dutiful wife, and as a person who receives divine visions that are typically reserved only for worthy and righteous figures in contemporary Qumranic, Pseudepigraphic and Merkavah Jewish literature. Daphna Arbel proposes that this alternative representation of Eve is subversive. It inverts the dominant characterizations of Eve as a sinner while associating her with notions that are considered theologically and socially honorable and praiseworthy.[48]

In *GLAE* 14:3 Adam asks her to teach their children the value of submitting to God's right way: "Call all our children and the children of our children and tell them the manner of our transgression." In another scene Eve is presented as a wise instructor: "Now, then, my children, I have shown you the way in which we were deceived; and do guard yourselves from transgressing against the good" (30:3). In other scenes she warns against obeying the voice of someone other than God (17:2; 21:5), succumbing to flattery (16:2–3; 18:1), being enticed by outward appearances (17:1; 18:5), and allowing an initial fear of offending God to be overcome (16:4a; 18:2; 21:4). This representation of Eve resonates with several features that are associated with the personified figure of Wisdom in the wisdom traditions, and thus characterizes Eve as an ethical person.[49]

Greek Life of Adam and Eve 32:2–3 pictures Eve having divine visions of transcendent worlds that are typically reserved for holy and ideal figures in Jewish theology and literature. For example, Eve sees the assumption of Adam's spirit to heaven via a chariot of light borne by four bright eagles descending to the place where Adam is lying after his death. The vision stands in the chariot-throne tradition of Ezekiel. It associates

46. Johnson, *Apoc Mos* 19.3, Charlesworth, *OTP*, vol. 2, 279.

47. Ibid., 283.

48. Arbel., et al., "And So They Went," 11–12.

49. Ibid., 15–18.

Eve with a long line of righteous male "ideal figures" who were considered worthy of such sublime visions. At the same time it subverts the dominant interpretations of Eve's materiality, carnality, and illicit sexuality. Eve is a privileged person with superior status and spirituality.[50]

The picture of Eve in *GLAE* and *Apoc Mos* is multivocal. Why two versions of Eve's story? Dietmar Neufeld proposes that the two perspectives reflect two different world views, the world view of males and the world view of females in the honor/shame culture of the ancient world. But that argument takes us beyond the focus of this book.[51]

SUMMARY OF THE ADAM/SIN STORY IN SECOND TEMPLE JUDAISM

The diversity of the Adam/sin story in Second Temple Judaism is stunning.

1. Adam in the Wisdom Literature is a heroic figure. He is a wise man. Adam is the first patriarch of the Jewish people (*Sirach, Wisdom of Solomon, Jubilees, Dead Sea Scrolls*). He is not the father of sin nor the origin of death.

2. The story of sin in much of this literature begins with Cain (*Sirach, Wisdom of Solomon*), or with the "marriage" of "the sons of God" and "the daughters of men" in Genesis 6 (*1 Enoch, Jubilees, Testament of the Twelve Patriarchs, Dead Sea Scrolls*). Or, God is responsible for the creation of an evil spirit in Genesis 1, and this evil spirit is responsible for sin (*The Community Rule* of the Dead Sea Scrolls).

3. There is a tradition that the animals lost the power of speech due to Adam and Eve's transgression in the garden (*Jubilees*, Philo, Josephus).

4. There is a tradition that faults Eve more than Adam for disobeying God in the Garden (*Jubilees*, Josephus, *Life of Adam and Eve*). And in one document illicit sexual desire becomes associated with Eve's transgression (*Life of Adam and Eve*).

5. One subversive tradition presents Eve as a virtuous and moral model who receives transcendent visions reserved for Judaism's most holy people (*Life of Adam and Eve*).

6. The apocalyptic writers attribute death, and the physical pain and chaos of the present evil age to Adam's transgression in the Garden (*4 Ezra, 2 Baruch*). But both reject the idea of hereditary sin or what later Christian theology would call "original sin."

50. Ibid., 19–21.

51. Neufeld in ibid., 47ff.

What seems clear is that the story of Adam and Eve's disobedience in the Garden receives significant interpretive attention in the 400 years of Second Temple Judaism (200 BCE—200 CE). But there is a significant divergence of interpretation about the meaning of the events reported in Genesis 3. In the earlier literature from this period Adam is a model of holiness and law observance, sometimes even before the giving of the law. In Jubilees Adam functions as a priest following his and Eve's transgression of God's commandment; he offers sin offerings before leaving the Garden (notice "leaving," not driven from the Garden).

The re-telling of the story fundamentally changes with the destruction of Jerusalem and the Temple in 70 CE. The Apocalyptic writers hold Adam, not Eve (only *2 Bar* 19:8 and 48:42 mention her), accountable for introducing sin into the world. The consequence of sin is universal death. To sin or not to sin, however, is a matter of individual responsibility. The unequivocal rejection of hereditary sinfulness in this literature does suggest that some people or groups contemporaneous with the writers were making the case for the hereditary transmission of sin from Adam as a way to explain the problem of evil in the world. The writers of *4 Ezra* and *2 Baruch* say a clear "no" to that theology around the turn of the first to second century CE.

When Adam and Even are held accountable for sin in the Garden of Eden in Second Temple Judaism, which is not universal, the consequence of their sin continues to be defined in relational categories. Sin is an act of the free will that disrupts relationships in history, including in nature (e.g., the animals can no longer speak with each other). But more than that, the sin of Adam and Eve has cosmic historic consequences, it effects a change in the apocalyptic ages by introducing the present evil age. While it would appear that a minority of people following the cataclysmic events 70 CE claimed that the sin of Adam and Eve effected an ontological change that was transmitted from generation to generation, the literature we have categorically rejects that interpretation (to use the telephone analogy, we assume the strong rejection of the ontological interpretation means that someone on the other end of the phone conversation was suggesting that, but we do not know for sure). What we do know for certain is that Second Temple Judaism believed in a relational understanding of sin—it is disobedient action which people freely chose to do—rather than the result of an ontological condition of human nature inherited from previous generations. In other words, the sin of Adam and Eve was interpreted in Second Temple Judaism in Jewish categories of thought—relational or covenantal rather than ontological.

3

The Story of Sin in the Jesus Movement: Paul the Follower of Jesus

JESUS AND THE MESSIANIC community that emerged following his death and resurrection with one exception showed little interest in the Adam and Eve narrative from Genesis 3. Only three out of twenty-seven writings in the New Testament canon make reference to the Adam and Eve story. But those references have become profoundly influential in the development of Christian thought.

One follower of Jesus, a Jewish man named Paul, was called by Jesus and the leaders of the early messianic community to serve as a missionary to the Gentiles. After establishing small house churches in various major centers of the Roman Empire, Paul wrote letters to some of these communities to pastors them regarding local issues facing the new believers in these churches. One such letter, 1 Corinthians, was written in 53–54 CE to several house churches in the city of Corinth.[1] In the process of answering some questions about the resurrection among members of these house churches, Paul asserted that "for as in Adam all die, so also in Christ shall all be made alive" (1 Cor 15:22). There is a parallelism between Adam and

---

1. See Collins, *First Corinthians*, 24; Hays, *First Corinthians*, 4; Witherington, *Conflict and Community in Corinth*, 73.

Christ: whatever happened in Adam is reversed in Christ. Paul provides no explanation of what he means by "in Adam all die."

Several years later, between late 55 and early 57 CE, Paul wrote another letter, this one to the house churches in the city of Rome, the capital of the Roman Empire.[2] There he states that

> therefore, as *sin* entered into the world through one man and through *sin* death, so also the death spread to all human beings *because all human beings sinned* (v. 12) . . . not as the transgression [false step], so also the gracious gift; for if by the transgression of one person, the many died, how much more the grace of God even the free gift in the grace of the one person Messiah Jesus abounded to the many (v. 15). . . . So then, just as through one transgression [there is] condemnation for all human beings, so also through one righteous act [there is] righteous life for all human beings (v 18). For just as through the disobedience of one person the many were made sinners, so also through the obedience of one the many will be made righteous. . . (v. 19) (Rom 5:12–19) [translation is mine].

Both of these letters were written a decade and a half before the destruction of Jerusalem and the Temple, but Paul makes the same apocalyptic Adam—death association that is made by *4 Ezra* and *2 Baruch* thirty years after 70 CE. He also held Adam accountable for introducing sin into the world ("*sin* entered the world through one man and through *sin* death"), and he underlines human responsibility for sin ("*because all human beings sinned*"). Paul's letters are written approximately fifty years before *4 Ezra* and *2 Baruch* but they reflect a similar apocalyptic theology while standing in front of the destruction of Jerusalem and the Temple rather than searching for a theodicy that will explain that historical and theological tragedy. Why does Paul seem to be breathing the same apocalyptic air as *4 Ezra* and *2 Baruch*?

FRAMING APOCALYPTIC THEOLOGY

Jewish apocalyptic theology began to emerge in some of the later prophetic writings of the Hebrew Scriptures (e.g., Isaiah 40–66, Ezekiel, Zechariah, Daniel) and came into full blossom in the literature of Second Temple Judaism (e.g., *1 Enoch, The War Scroll* of the Dead Sea Scrolls, *4 Ezra,*

---

2. See Dunn, *Romans*, Vol. 1, xliii; Jewett, *Romans*, 22–23; Toews, *Romans*, 20.

2 Baruch, The Apocalypse of Abraham).[3] This theology asserts that God enters or invades history and fundamentally disorients and changes the course of history. The theology is characterized by the dualistic doctrine of "two ages"—"the present evil age" and "the age to come." There is no continuity between these two ages. At some future moment "the age to come" will break into the human realm by a supernatural act of God in which evil will be annihilated and the righteous will be redeemed. History looks like this:

God's Intervention
Present Age | Age to Come

PAUL'S REFRAMING

Paul's theology is fundamentally an apocalyptic theology that is reframed in light of the life, death, and resurrection of Messiah Jesus. Paul modified Jewish apocalyptic theology in both directions—moving backward and forward.

1) Paul believes that Adam's transgression in Genesis 3 introduced the Present Evil Age. Adam's sin was due to an apocalyptic event. The serpent (not called Satan in Gen 3 or Rom 5) symbolized an apocalyptic agent who introduces *Sin (hamartia)* as power. *Sin* in Romans 5 is singular and is about apocalyptic power, *not* sins as acts.

2) Christ's death is interpreted by Paul as an apocalyptic event/invasion by God. Paul asserts in Romans 8:32 that God handed Jesus over to anti-god apocalyptic powers to bring about his crucifixion, thereby setting in motion their final defeat. The cross is not simply an expression of the love of God, but a unique and determinative apocalyptic event in the struggle between God and the anti-god powers of the cosmos.[4] This interpretation of Romans 8:32 is supported by Romans 3:21–26 when the phrase *dia pisteos Iesou Xristou* is interpreted as "the faith*fulness of* Messiah Jesus" rather than "faith *in* Jesus."[5]

3) God's raising Jesus from the dead is an apocalyptic event. The resurrection of Jesus was an apocalyptic event which signaled the beginning of the general resurrection, the beginning of the age to come. It proclaimed

---

3. See Collins, *Apocalyptic Imagination*; Nickelsburg, *Ancient Judaism.*.

4. See Gaventa, "Interpreting the Death of Jesus Apocalyptically," 125–45.

5. See Toews, *Romans*, 99–113.

that Jesus was God's eschatological Messiah, that Jesus was the bringer of God's eschatological salvation for Israel and all people.

Paul's interpretation of history is genuinely apocalyptic. The entrance of *Sin* into history through the transgression of Adam introduced an apocalyptic power, a cosmic anti-god figure, a ruler figure. Messiah Jesus' life, death and resurrection was God's apocalyptic answer to the apocalyptic power of *Sin* introduced by Adam into the world. History is really about two apocalyptic paradigmatic figures, Adam and Jesus. The life, death, and resurrection of Jesus was the apocalyptic event for Paul that the destruction of Jerusalem and the Temple was for *4 Ezra* and *2 Baruch* with one critical difference. The writers of *4 Ezra* and *2 Baruch* were trying to formulate a theodicy so that they and their people could hope again. Paul believed that the apocalyptic events of Jesus' life, death, and resurrection meant history now existed at the "mingling of the ages" (1 Cor 10:11 especially, and 2 Cor 5:16), that is, the overlap of the present evil age and the age to come. History now looked like this:

God's Intervention

Cross/resurrection   Parousia

Present Evil Age | End of Ages | New Creation

Jesus by his faithfulness to the promises of God to Israel and to the world had defeated the apocalyptic powers of *Sin* (also called "principalities and power," "rulers," "dominions," "thrones") and inaugurated "the age to come" (see Rom 3:22, 26; Gal 2:16 [x2], 2:20, 3:22, 26; Phil 3:19; Eph 3:12).[6] The "new creation" had been guaranteed for Paul because the power of *Sin* had been defeated in the death and resurrection of Jesus (Rom 4:25; 8:18–25; 31–9; 2 Cor 1:20; Gal 1:4; 1 Cor 15:53–57).[7]

PAUL'S APOCALYPTIC THEOLOGY OF SIN

Paul personifies *Sin* in the Romans texts on *Sin* (set in *italics* to make this clear). *Sin* is singular. It is *Sin* as power, as reign, as magnetic field. *Sin* is a

6. See Toews, *Romans*, 101–11 for the exegetical basis for this interpretation, and the bibliography listed there plus now also Bird and Sprinkle, *The Faith of Jesus Christ*; and Easter, "The Pistis Christou Debate," 33–47.

7. For an exposition of Paul's theology from this apocalyptic theological perspective, see Beker, *Paul the Apostle*; Beker, *Paul's Apocalyptic Gospel*; Beker, *The Triumph of God*; de Boer, *The Defeat of Death*, 140–80; Brown, *The Cross and Human Transformation*; Adams, *Constructing the World*, 130–49; Wright, *Paul*, 40–58; Thiselton, *The Living Paul*, 11–19.

personal power; it has desires and passions (6:12; 7:5); it is opportunistic (7:8, 11); it revives from sleep (7:9); it deceives (7:11); it dwells within (7:17, 20, 23). As a personal power, it enters the world (5:12); it rules (5:21; 6:12, 13, 14); it enslaves (6:6, 16, 17, 20; 7:14; 8:2); it works (7:17, 20); it has its own law (7:12—8.2). Paul interprets *Sin* as a cosmic power.

Sin as cosmic power was present in the cosmos before Adam. It strode onto the stage of human history through one person. The one person is not identified in the text, but reference to Adam is unmistakable for Paul and his audience, as v. 14 indicates. Adam turned *Sin* loose in the world. And with *Sin* came *Death*, also personified in Romans.

Sin as cosmic power in the world is the legacy of Adam seen as the universal patriarch. As cosmic power, *Sin* pulls all human beings, except Jesus, and all creation into its magnetic force field. Nothing is capable of bounding its power or freeing people or creation from its pull, not even the gift of God's revealed law. *Sin* is Cosmic King in Paul. *Sin's* kingship is total, with the one exception of Jesus; no one and nothing can escape its tyrannical rule. It exists and rules even when there is no system to define it, when it cannot be counted or tracked.

The categories of interpretation are Jewish apocalyptic theology. The reality of the present world is that it is ruled by the evil power of *Sin*. Where *Sin* came from Paul never discusses, nor does he discuss how *Sin* and *Death* became linked. He, like his fellow Jewish apocalyptic theologians, just assume that death is the consequence of *Sin*.

Given this apocalyptic theology of *Sin*, Paul says two things that seem contradictory but were not for him nor his fellow Jewish apocalyptists. First, all human beings are under the rule of *Sin* (Rom 3:9)—there is universal sin because of the cosmic power of *Sin*. Second, all humans are responsible for the spread of death "because all sin" (Rom 5:12)—there is individual human responsibility for sinful behavior; that is, all humans, except one (Jesus), choose to submit to *Sin's* rule by behaving sinfully. The exception of the one person's obedience is critical; it underlines free choice and human responsibility. Jesus entered the world ruled by *Sin* but chose not to submit; instead his obedience both demonstrated and effected the saving power to overcome *Death* with *Life*.[8]

8. The discussion of Paul's apocalyptic theology of sin follows the analysis in Toews, *Romans*, 155–67; 409–11.

WHY PAUL'S APOCALYPTIC REFRAMING?

Paul reframes his understanding of *Sin* for two reasons. First, Paul genuinely believed that Jesus was the Jewish Messiah who was bringing to fulfillment the promises of Israel's Scriptures: he was liberating and would liberate Israel and the nations from oppression, including enslavement to the power of *Sin*, and bring God's salvation to all nations. Secondly, as Paul so clearly states in the thesis of the letter (1:16–18), Romans was about the good news of God's salvation to the Jews and the Gentiles equally. Paul was saying to the relatively young house churches composed of Jewish and Gentile believers in the capital of the Roman Empire that salvation and righteousness was theirs through Messiah Jesus, not through Caesar Augustus. The answer to the problem of *Sin* [*scelus* in Latin], which, according to chapters 14–15, was fracturing relationships within the house churches, and which, according to Roman imperial propaganda was threatening the unity of the empire, was to be found in Messiah Jesus not in Caesar Augustus as proclaimed by the agents of the Roman emperor. *Sin* is mentioned forty-one of forty-five times in chapters 5–8 in Romans, precisely the chapters where Paul describes the nature of the salvation that God offers through "the faithfulness of Messiah of Jesus" proclaimed in 3:21–26.[9]

Paul "apocalyptizes" *Sin* in Romans not to develop a universal theology of sin, but to argue 1) that *all* people, Jews and Gentiles equally, are under the power of *Sin*, 2) that Messiah Jesus "makes right" and liberates Jews and Gentiles equally from the power of *Sin*, 3) that salvation, peace, and righteousness through Messiah Jesus answers the problem of *Sin* that is fracturing the relationships of Jewish and Gentile believers. As Paul states so clearly in the whole of the Romans 5:12–21 text, an apocalyptic understanding of Messiah Jesus requires an apocalyptic understanding of Adam's sin. An apocalyptic Adam is a necessary foil to an apocalyptic Messiah Jesus in Romans 5.

WHAT ABOUT EVE?

Paul's apocalyptic theology of *Sin* focuses on Adam. Eve is not mentioned in the 1 Corinthians and Romans comparisons of Adam and Christ. Paul

9. See Stendahl, "The Apostle Paul and the Introspective Conscience of the West," 78–96; Toews, *Romans*, 50–64, 99–113, 150–67, 332–49; Toews, "Righteousness in Romans," 209–22. See also Carter, *Paul and the Power of Sin*, for an interesting sociological analysis.

references Eve twice but in a quite different way than Adam. First, Paul refers to Eve's deception by the serpent's cunning in 2 Corinthians 11:3, but he is warning about the cunning deception of other preachers who preach a different gospel than Paul. He expresses his concern via the metaphor of an engagement. The engagement between the future bride (the Corinthian house churches as a whole) and the future husband (Christ) has been negotiated by Paul. According to Jewish tradition, the engagement means an exclusive linkage of the woman (here the Corinthian community) to the future bridegroom (here Christ) until the two are married and she moves into his house to live with him (Deut 22:13–21). Paul is expressing a fear that the community, which he considered to be a true virgin, is facing the danger during the intermediary time between the engagement and the marriage of being tempted by the false preachers to follow another gospel. It is at this point in his narrative that the comparison with Eve is used. His concern is not Eve's disobedience of God's command in the Garden and thus not the question of sin. What is important though is that Paul is familiar with an interpretive tradition that intensifies the meaning of "deceived" in Genesis 3:13. The LXX of Genesis 3:13 reads, "and the woman said, 'the serpent deceived [epatesen] me . . .'" Paul here uses a compound form of the verb, exepatesen, which intensifies the meaning, "really deceived."[10] A point of debate among scholars is whether Paul's reference to the Genesis 3:13 text carries an erotic-sexual connotation, as it did in some later Jewish apocalyptic texts (Apoc. Ab. 23) and rabbinic sources ('Abod. Zar. 22b; B. Sabb. 145b–46a; Yebam. 103b) in which the serpent was believed to have had sexual intercourse with Eve?[11] A major problem with the "erotic-sexual" interpretation is the dating of the Jewish "parallel texts." The Apocalypse of Abraham is a late first century text,[12] and the rabbinic midrashic texts are assumed to be a good bit later than Paul but are impossible to date with any precision.[13] Secondly, the contexts in which the parallels texts are located are very different than 2 Corinthians 11:3. As Samuel Sandmel taught us many years ago, parallel texts or similar language used in different contexts mean different things.[14] Third,

10. See Furnish, II Corinthians, 486–87; Harris, Second Epistle to the Corinthians, 740.

11. E.g., Kuechler, Schweigen, Schmuck und Schleier, 41–44, who favors such a reading, versus Martin, 2 Corinthians, 333, and Lambrecht, Second Corinthians, 173, who are skeptical.

12. See Rubinkiewicz, "Apocalypse of Abraham," Vol. 1, 683.

13. van Oyen, "The Character of Eve," 19.

14. Sandmel, "Parallelomania," 1–13.

as Geert van Oyen points out, Adam is not mentioned anywhere in the 2 Corinthians 11 text. The issue is not adultery in relationship to Adam, but the potential of creating distance between the Corinthian communities and Christ. A more likely comparison, van Oyen suggests, is the potential of unfaithful behavior on the part of the community in the metaphor of the wedding between the people and their Lord from Isaiah 54:5.[15]

The second reference to Eve by Paul or a disciple of Paul, depending on your view of the authorship of 1 Timothy, is 1 Timothy 2:14, "Adam was not deceived, but the woman was really deceived and became a transgressor."[16] The simple form of the word "deceived" is used for Adam, but, as in 2 Corinthians 11:3, the intensified form "really deceived" is used of Eve. The differences with the 2 Corinthians text are noteworthy. Eve and Adam are clearly differentiated. Eve was "really deceived," but Adam was not. Second, Eve became a transgressor; she literally "stepped across the line" or she "mis-stepped." Paul or his circle of disciples were familiar with a Jewish tradition that said Eve was more easily deceived by the serpent than Adam, and that women were more susceptible to deception than men.[17] Paul or his disciple used this distinction as a rationale to support his exhortation that a woman should learn in silence rather than teach. Only childbearing could save the woman provided she continued in faith, love, holiness and modesty (v. 15).

The differentiation of Eve from Adam in 1 Timothy is part of a larger tradition in Second Temple Judaism as is evident in the re-telling of the Genesis 1–3 narrative in the book of *Jubilees*, second century BCE, and the *Life of Adam and Eve*, late first century or early second century CE. In this tradition there is both a degradation of Eve, she is inferior to Adam, and a blaming of her for the disobedience in the Garden. For example, in *Jubilees* Eve is not permitted to enter the Garden for eighty days after her creation, which is forty days later than Adam (3:9–12). Or, again in *Jubilees* Eve covers "her shame" with a fig leaf before she gives the fruit of the tree to Adam to eat. Or, in the *Life of Adam and Eve* the book begins with Eve saying to Adam, "My Lord, would you kill me? O that I would die! Then perhaps the

15. Van Oyen, "The Character of Eve," 19–20.

16. See Johnson, *Letters to Paul's Delegates*, 1–33; Johnson, *The Writings of the New Testament*, 423–52; and Towner, *The Letters of Timothy and Titus*, 1–89, for careful summaries of the debate and bibliography re the authorship of 1 Timothy.

17. See Johnson, *Delegates*, 139–41; Towner, *Letters*, 228–33; Marshall and Towner, *Pastoral Epistles*, 463–67; Collins, *1 and 2 Timothy and Titus*, 71.

Lord God will bring you again into Paradise, for it is because of me that the Lord God is angry with you" (1:3).[18]

Eve was deceived and stepped across the boundary or acted sinfully. But Eve's transgression is not interpreted as an apocalyptic event in the way that Adam's was. For Paul, Adam's transgression changed history in a way that Eve's did not. Adam's transgression introduced the present evil age by letting lose the power of *Sin* which was so powerful that it enslaved all human beings, except one (Jesus), and all creation.

SUMMARY OF PAUL'S THEOLOGY OF SIN

1. Paul transformed Adam's transgression in the Garden into an apocalyptic event. The turning point of history is located in Genesis 3, not Genesis 6 as in the *Book of the Watchers* of 1 Enoch, or in Genesis 1 as in the *Treatise of the Two Spirits* of *The Community Rule*.

2. Paul believed that Adam's transgression introduced an apocalyptic power into history that ruled the cosmos and enslaved all humans and all creation. Paul believed in universal, cosmic sinfulness.

3. Paul linked Adam's introduction of *Sin* into the world and the death of all human beings. The consequence of sin is mortality.

4. Paul taught that all human beings are responsible for their own sinful behavior. Paul believed in individual responsibility.

5. Paul or his circle of disciples were aware of a tradition that viewed Eve as more susceptible to temptation than Adam.

6. Paul was not concerned with the transmission of sin, nor did he teach any kind of hereditary sinfulness or what later Christian theology called "original sin." Universal sinfulness in Paul had to do with the cosmic power or rulership of *Sin* rather than the biological transmission of sin from one generation to the next.

Sin in Paul is defined as a relational problem, or quite literally a political problem, the rulership of *Sin*, from which human beings and creation need liberation. Sin is not defined in ontological categories. Paul outlines a political theology of sin, not a metaphysical doctrine of sin. And, it should be noted, Paul never identifies this apocalyptical power of *Sin* with a personal Satan.

18. See van Oyen, "The Character of Eve," 24–25, who suggests that this differentiation of Eve from Adam is part of a larger body/spirit dualism that is developing in Judaism from the second century BCE forward in which women are associated with the body and men with the spirit.

We have now traced the story of sin through the Bible and the literature written between and around the Hebrew Scriptures and what ultimately became the New Testament canon. We still have not found the ontological theology of sin that I was taught in the church and in college.

4

The Story of Original Sin in the Greek Church Fathers (ca. 150–400 CE)

THE ROMAN EMPIRE WAS divided by two primary cultures and languages—Greek east of Italy and Egypt, Latin from Italy west—even
though Latin was the official language of the Empire. The early Christian
movement began in the eastern part of the Roman Empire. The majority of
congregations to begin with were in Palestine, Syria, Asia Minor (Turkey
today), and Greece. Thus the predominant language of the early Christian
missionary movement was Greek. All of writings in the New Testament
were written in Greek. Even when the Christian movement moved west
into Italy and Gaul (France today), including the capital city of Rome
where the official language was Latin, the language of the Christian movement remained Greek because the earliest Christians there were Greek
speaking immigrants from the east, primarily from Asia Minor. Therefore,
the writings that we have from the earliest post-apostolic Christian leaders
are in Greek, e.g., Clement of Rome, Justin Martyr writing from Rome,
Irenaeus writing from Gaul.

The earliest church leaders who address the transgression of Adam
in Genesis 3 or Paul's interpretation of Adam's sin in Romans 5 come
from the Greek speaking eastern fathers. It is not until the end of the
second century that we find a reference to Adam's transgression from
a Latin speaking church leader. But more than language is at stake. The

Greek speaking eastern fathers have a more optimistic view of human nature than do the Latin speaking church fathers, a reality which is reflected to this day in the different theologies of sin and salvation between the Eastern Orthodox Church and the Western Roman Catholic and Protestant Churches.

We have no reference in early Christian writings of Adam's transgression in the Garden from Paul's Letter to the Romans, mid-first century CE, until the writings of Justin Martyr, mid-second century CE. That is, a whole series of important early second century church leaders known as "the Apostolic Fathers" because of their close connections with the last of the apostles of Jesus—Clement of Rome, Ignatius, Papias, Polycarp, Barnabas, the anonymous writers of the Didache and the Shepherd of Hermas—make no reference to the Genesis 3 narrative. They are proclaiming the gospel, establishing new churches, ordering the life of existing churches, trying to resolve disputes and leadership rebellions in existing churches, and exhorting fairly new Christians about appropriate ethical behavior in a pagan world, but do not think it important to write their congregations about the disobedience and sin of Adam and Eve.

JUSTIN MARTYR (D. CA. 165 CE)

It is the middle of the second century in the city of Rome before an apologist for the Christian faith, Justin Martyr, in a conversation with a Jewish person makes the first post-Pauline reference to the Genesis 3 story. Justin is clear that Adam's transgression of God's command, to which Adam was seduced by the serpent-devil, placed the human race under a curse.[1] But he is equally clear that there is no inheritance of sin; each person is responsible for his or her own sins:

> The Christ has suffered to be crucified for the race of men who, since Adam, were fallen to the power of death and were in the error of the serpent, each man committing evil by his own fault.
>
> Men . . . were created like God, free from pain and death, provided they obeyed His precepts and were deemed worthy by Him to be called His sons, and yet, like Adam and Eve, brought death upon themselves. . . . [T]hey were considered worthy to become gods, and to have the capability of becoming Sons of

---

1. Justin Martyr, *Dialogue with Trypho*, 94, Vol. 6.

the Most High, yet each is to be judged and convicted, as were Adam and Eve.[2]

As Peter Bouteneff states, Adam may be the protosinner, but Justin makes plain that sin by subsequent humans is entirely a matter of human free choice.[3]

THEOPHILUS OF ANTIOCH

About twenty years after Justin Martyr another Christian apologist Theophilus from Antioch, about whom we know very little, wrote a letter to Autolycus (ca. 180 CE). Theophilus in this letter introduced an interpretation of the Adam and Eve story which became very influential in the eastern churches. Adam and Eve's disobedience, he said, was due to their mental and spiritual immaturity. This is what he said:

> The tree of knowledge itself was good . . . knowledge is good when one uses it discreetly. But Adam, being yet an infant in age, was on this account as yet unable to receive knowledge worthily. For now, also, when a child is born it is not at once able to eat bread, but is nourished first with milk, and then, with the increment of years, it advances to solid food. Thus, too, would it have been with Adam; for not, as one who begrudged him, as some suppose, did God command him not to eat of knowledge. But he wished also to make proof of him, whether he was submissive to His commandment. . . . [I]f it is right that children be subject to parents, how much more to the God and Father of all things? . . . [F]or the first man, disobedience procured his expulsion from Paradise. Not, therefore, as if there were any evil in the tree of knowledge; but from his disobedience did man draw, as from a fountain, labour, pain, grief, and at last all prey to death.[4]

> And God showed great kindness to man in this, that He did not suffer man to remain in sin for ever . . . just as a vessel, when on being fashioned it has some flaw, is remoulded or remade, that it may become new and entire; so also happens to man by death.

---

2. Ibid., 124.

3. Bouteneff, *Beginnings*, 62; see also Kelly, *Early Christian Doctrines*, 166–68; Weaver, "From Paul to Augustine," 189–90.

4. Theophilus to Autolycus, xxv.

> For somehow or other he is broken up, that he may rise in the resurrection whole.[5]

> Man was by nature neither mortal nor immortal. He would have gained immortality as a reward for keeping the commandments of God; he would thus become God. If, however, man disobeyed the commandments of God he would become the cause of death. God made man free with power over himself.[6]

Adam's problem, according to Theophilus, was that he was a child, *nepios*. He and Eve partook of a good thing too early, before they were ready for it. Theophilus did not spell out the consequences of Adam and Eve's transgression on the rest of humanity, but he planted a very important seed.[7]

IRENAEUS OF LYONS (CA. 140–200 CE)

Theophilus' interpretation was seminal for Irenaeus, the most important and influential Christian theologian of the second century. Like so many of the early Christian church leaders, we know little about Irenaeus apart from his writings. He came from Smyrna in Asia Minor (Turkey today) and had associations with Bishop Polycarp of Smyrna who was a disciple of the Apostle John.[8] Like many other Greeks from Asia Minor Irenaeus moved to the Rhone River valley, but then escaped the persecutions ordered by the emperor Marcus Aurelius on the Christians of Lyon and Vienne in 177. Upon his return to Lyon, Irenaeus was elected bishop of the church to replace Photinus who had been martyred.[9]

As Bishop of Lyon Irenaeus wrote a defense of one understanding of the Christian faith against a movement known as Gnosticism. Irenaeus articulation of the Christian faith became the basis for what later became known as "orthodox Christianity." The primary defense of Irenaeus is a book known as *Against Heresies* (*AH* hereafter), written between 177–85. A second work, *Proof of the Apostolic Preaching*, was written ten to fifteen years after *AH* near the end of Irenaeus' life.[10] If the first work is an

5. Ibid., xxvi.

6. Ibid., xxvii.

7. See also Kelly, *Early Christian Doctrines*, 168.

8. See Irenaeus, *Against Heresies*, Vol. 1, iii,3.4.

9. See Chadwick, *The Church in Ancient Society*, 100; and Quasten, *Patrology*, Vol. 1, 287–88, for the brief biographical information on Irenaeus.

10. See Irenaeus, *Proof of the Apostolic Preaching*, Vol. 16, 6.

apologetic against the gnostics, the second is "a compendium of theology,"[11] as Irenaeus understood it. In both *AH* and *Proofs* Irenaeus developed and amplified Theophilus' reading of the Genesis story of Adam and Eve as children, *nepioi*, in the Garden; they were imperfect, undeveloped, and infantile persons.[12] The picture in *Proofs* is typical:

> And Adam and Eve . . . were naked and were not ashamed, for their thoughts were innocent and childlike, and they had no conception or imagination of the sort that is engendered in the soul by evil, through concupiscence, and by lust. For they were then in their integrity, preserving their natural state. . . . [N]ow, so long as the spirit remains in proper order and vigour, it is without imagination or conception of what is shameful. For this reason they were not ashamed, and they kissed each other and embraced with the innocence of childhood.[13]

Adam and Eve were created in the "image (*eikon*) and likeness (*homoiosis*) of God," but these were present like a germ that was to develop slowly through the possession of the Spirit and fellowship with God.[14] This goal of moral, spiritual, and intellectual maturity was to be attained through a period of long development.[15] Their sin was that they partook of the knowledge of the tree of good and evil before they were mature and ready for the knowledge.[16] It was "a moral mistake attributable to the spiritual and intellectual immaturity of Adam and Eve."[17] The punishment for Adam and Eve's disobedience was death and the loss of the likeness of God, but not the image of God.[18] The latter was God's eternal goal for humanity even before creation in the person of Jesus Christ.

In addition to his conviction that Adam and Eve were children when they disobeyed God, Irenaeus believed that human beings from the beginning possessed free will and were endowed with the ability to make choices. That is, God made humans free agents. There is no coercion with

11. Smith's phrase, Ibid., 19.

12. *AH*, ix, lxii.

13. *Proof*, Λ, 14.

14. *AH.*, iv lxiv, vi.

15. Ibid., iv, lxiii.

16. For a very similar reading of Irenaeus, see Bouteneff, *Beginnings*, 77–85; Kelly, *Early Christian Doctrines*, 170–74; Weaver, "Paul to Augustine," 191–92; Steenberg, "Children in Paradise," 1–22; Williams, *Ideas of the Fall*, 189–99; Tennant, Sources, 283–91.

17. Downing, "The Doctrine of Regeneration," 99–112.

18. See *AH* iii.18.1; v.2.1; v.21.3; and Kelly, *Early Christian Doctrines*, 171.

God; "in man, as well as in angels, He has placed the power of choice . . ."[19] A little later Irenaeus repeats the same point by asserting that humans are endowed with the faculty of distinguishing good and evil; they have the power of their will to choose to perform God's commandments.[20]

Adam's first sin was one of thoughtlessness rather than of malice. The primary blame for Adam's misstep rests with the devil who acquired power over him unfairly, by a trick.[21] It is not surprising that Irenaeus did not attach a high degree of guilt or culpability to Adam's sin. God pitied, rather than condemned, his frail, imperfect, inexperienced creature for succumbing to the wiles of a cunning and powerful foe.[22] The sin of Adam was far less serious than Cain's.[23] Adam's transgression, though not an infection transmitted to subsequent generations, did lead to death, which Irenaeus also interpreted as a divine mercy.[24]

Norman Williams in his 1924 Brampton Lectures observes that closely connected with these ideas is the even more startling speculation that Adam's sin was in some ways positively beneficial to humankind; "it almost becomes what has been called a 'Fall upwards,' inasmuch as it conduced to man's fuller and richer ethical evolution. . . . [M]an learnt from painful experience that sin brings separation from God and spiritual death."[25]

Williams suggests that by the late second century in the Greek speaking eastern church we have "a picture of primitive man as frail, imperfect, and child-like. . . . It finds in the inherited disorder of our nature rather a weakness to be pitied than an offence to be condemned . . ."[26] Gustaf Wingren adds the important historical note that a theology of man's "original state" does not emerge until the late fourth and early fifth centuries; before that time "we find hardly any account of the first paradisiacal world and its perfect man."[27]

19. *AH*, iv, xxxvii.
20. Ibid., iv, xxxix.
21. Ibid., iii, xxxi.
22. Ibid., iii., xxv.
23. Ibid., iv; xxxviii; xl.
24. Ibid., iii.
25. Williams, *Ideas of the Fall*, 195. Williams based this observation on *AH*, iv, lxiv.
26. Ibid., p. 200.
27. Wingren, *Man and Incarnation*, 28.

CLEMENT OF ALEXANDRIA (150–215)

Alexandria, Egypt, was the second largest city in the Roman Empire. It had been a citadel of high Greek culture from the time of Alexander the Great onward. It became one of the major centers of eastern Christian intellectual and theological formation in the late second century and first half of the third century. A man by the name of Titus Flavius Clements, known in church history as Clement of Alexandria, established and headed a catechetical school in the city where he taught for twenty years.[28] During these twenty years he wrote three books, *Exhortation (Protreptikos)*, *Tutor (Paidagogos)*, *Miscellanies (Stromata)*. Clement, like Irenaeus, believed that Adam and Eve were child-like and innocent in the Garden, destined to mature by stages toward perfection. Progress toward the goal of maturity depended on the exercise of free-will.[29] The fault of Adam and Eve was that they used their free will incorrectly; they indulged in the pleasures of sexual intercourse before God granted them permission.[30] Sex itself was not wrong, as many gnostics suggested, but the violation of God's ordinance was. As a result Adam and Eve lost the immortal life of Paradise and became prey to sinful passions.[31] Note should be made here of the tendency to assign a sexual character to the first sin, a characteristic that will increase as we move through the patristic period. In contrast to later interpretations, the wickedness of the act consisted not in its sexual nature, but in its prematureness.[32]

A second important theme in Clement, which is expanded in his student Origen, is that Adam and the human race are identified as one entity. Adam's name, which means humanity, is interpreted allegorically to mean universal man rather than an individual historical person.[33] In one passage Clement explicitly, "scornfully" according to Williams, rejects the idea of "original sin":

> Let them tell us, where the newly born child committed fornication, or how a thing that has performed no action at all has fallen under the curse of Adam? . . . And when David says "I was conceived in sins and in iniquities did my mother bear me," he

28. *Stromata*, iii, xii, xv, xviii.

29. *Stromata*, iv, xxiii; vi, xii; and *Protreptikos* xi, 1–2.

30. *Stromata*, iii, xii, xv, xvii.

31. Ibid., ii, xix.

32. See Bray, "Original Sin," 39; Kelly, *Early Christian Doctrines*, 179; Weaver, "Paul to Augustine," 193–94.

33. See Kelly, *Early Christian Doctrines*, 179; Williams, *Ideas of the Fall*, 203.

is alluding in prophetic wise to Eve as his mother; but Eve became the mother of all living, and even if David was "conceived in sin," yet he is not thereby involved in sin, nor indeed is he himself in sin.[34]

In another text, he explains that Job 1:21 ("Naked I came from my mother's womb . . .") means a child is born free from sin.[35]

Clement is clear that sin is an action freely chosen by human beings.[36] Sin is not brought about through the agency of demons for then the sinner would be guiltless. The only sinfulness of nature is that which results from individuals having become sinful through acts of sinning.[37] Clement explicitly rejects the traducian theory of the origin of the soul which was being taught by Tertullian at this time in Carthage, North Africa (see chapter 5). According to this theory, hereditary guilt is transmitted from generation to generation through sexual reproduction.[38]

ORIGEN (185/86–251/254)

Clement's successor in Alexandria was Origen, the second of the three great theologians in patristic Christianity (Irenaeus, Origen, Augustine). Origen was born into a Christian home in Alexandria, and given a thorough biblical and theological education by his father, Leonidas. When Clement fled Alexandria during the persecution of the emperor Severus (202 CE) in which Origen's father was martyred, Bishop Demetrius of Alexandria put Origen in charge of the catechetical school that Clement had founded even though Origen was only eighteen years old. Origen attracted many students to the school by the brilliance of his intellect and by the very disciplined quality of his personal life. Origen taught at the Alexandrian school for nearly thirty years, 202 to 231, before he moved to Caesarea in Palestine to establish another school. He traveled widely in the Roman world teaching in churches, consulting with the leading teachers of the time, and refuting heretics. He died in 253 because of sufferings endured during the persecutions of the emperor Decius.

---

34. *Stromata* iii, xvii; see also Tennant, *Sources*, 294–95; Williams, *Ideas of the Fall*, 207; and Kelly, *Early Christian Doctrines*, 179.

35. *Stromata* iv, xxv.

36. Ibid., iv.

37. *Stromata*, vi.12.

38. Ibid., vi, xvi. See also Tennant, *Sources*, 294–95.

Origen was a prolific writer. He wrote 2,000 books, commentaries, sermons, and treatises, according to the church father Jerome. Unfortunately most of his writings have been lost, and the few that we have are in Latin translation rather than in Greek. His major theological work, *On First Principles* (*De principiis*), was the first Christian system of theology. In this book Origen tried to explain the origin of evil within the framework of ethical monotheism. He treated the Genesis 3 narrative as an allegorical story of the collective fall of humanity in the transcendent world, a worldview he received from the Greek philosopher Plato. Adam did not represent an individual historical figure, according to Origen, but an allegory of humanity and the fall of humanity before history. The evils and injustices experienced in this life were due to transgressions committed in a previous, other worldly life; that is, Origen believed in the theory of a pre-natal or extra-temporal "fall" of individual souls. Origen represents the first Christian theological attempt to remove the origin of evil from the phenomenal world and place it in the transcendent world; his theory is the first form of the transcendental "Fall" doctrine.[39]

Origen's theory assumes a certain view of the creation of the soul, a much debated topic in Greco-Roman philosophy and among the early church fathers. Origen believed in the pre-existence of the soul. God created a pre-determined number of souls at some point in eternity. The degree of disobedience against God's ordinances in the transcendent world determined the level of fall into the temporal or material world— a mild rebellion resulted in a fall to angelic status, a radical rebellion resulted in a fall to demonic status, a moderate rebellion resulted in a fall to human status.

All humans (except Jesus) were prone to sin by nature because of transgressions in their pre-historical life. The fact that humans are sinful from birth has entirely to do with their pre-natal transgressions, not the disobedience of the first man, who in fact is simply an allegory of the pre-cosmic fall. Child baptism was necessary to wash away these pre-natal sins.

Origen wrote a commentary on Romans, probably some time between 244 and 249. Unfortunately we have access to only parts of Origen's exegesis through the garbled late fourth or early fifth century Latin translation of Rufinus (d. ca. 410). But as far as we can tell from the writings available to us, Origen was one of the few early church theologians to deal

---

39. See Tennant, *Sources*, 297; Williams, *Idea of the Fall*, 212–16; Kelly, *Early Christian Doctrines*, 180–81; Fredriksen, *Sin*, 100–112.

explicitly with Romans 5:12–21. He interprets the critical *eph ho* phrase ("because") of v. 12d in a causal way: "death has befallen all men *because* all have sinned." This exegesis, Henri Rondet notes, is that of the majority of the Greek fathers,[40] which is very different than Ambrosiaster's and Augustine's. Origen is clear that Adam's posterity suffered Adam's punishment, death, but at no point does he say that all humanity sinned in Adam. Origen is preoccupied with the cause of death, whether Adam's sin or one's own, rather than with the transmission of sin. For example, he says: "For all the men were in the loins of Adam when he was in paradise, and when he was expelled from it; thus, the death which came from his prevarication passed by him into all those who are of his blood; thus the apostle says: 'As all die in Adam, all will be resurrected in Christ.'"[41] Or:

> It is written that when Adam had sinned, the Lord banished him
> from the paradise of delights and that this punishments for his
> sin . . . passed on to all men. All, in fact, have been sent into this
> place of humiliation . . . whether all the sons of the sons of Adam
> were in his loins and were expelled with him from paradise, or
> whether each one of us was banished personally and received
> his condemnation in some way that we cannot tell and that only
> God knows.[42]

The first option refers to the theory of a metaphysical Adam who held all humanity spiritually in himself and who were fragmented in his fall. The second alternative probably refers to the theory of the fall of souls from the transcendent world into the material world.[43]

In his comment on Romans 5:15, Origen asks if Adam is the only cause of death by his sin, and answers that men become liable to death not so much from nature as from Adam's example.[44] Weaver proposes that Origen is "an extreme case of an attitude common to all the eastern fathers: 'no accountability without liberty.'"[45] Weaver goes on the assert that it offends Origen's "sense of justice that any person should be found in a corrupted, moral or sinful condition prior to his own free and willing

---

40. Rondet, *Original Sin*, 80.

41. *Commentary on Romans*, PG 14:1010, as quoted in Weaver, "Paul to Augustine," 196.

42. *Commentari Romanos*, v, col. 1029. Translation is by Rondet, *Original Sin*, 80.

43. See Rondet, *Original Sin*, 80.

44. See *Commentary on Romans*, PG 14:1024b, as translated in Weaver, "Paul to Augustine," 196.

45. Weaver, "Paul to Augustine," 196.

action, and his theory and allegorical interpretation of the fall of Adam as the pre-mundane fall of souls is a radical attempt to resolve the paradoxical situation of present culpability for a fault antecedent to one's existence."[46]

THE REACTION TO ORIGEN IN THE EAST

With a few exceptions, the history of Eastern thought on questions of Adam's sin and its consequences following Origen is in large measure a reaction toward the positions he took.

For example, Methodius, bishop of Olympus (260–311), a little town in Lycia (SW Turkey today), was a highly educated man and well trained theologian, who died a martyrs death in 311. He rejected the allegorical interpretation of Genesis 3, the pre-existence of the soul as well as the idea of pre-natal fall into the world of matter.[47] He, like his Greek predecessors, believed that Adam was overcome by evil while still an imperfect man, a babe. He also was strongly committed to human free will.

But Methodius made two notable contributions to the story of original sin. He was the first person to use the term "Fall" to describe the sin of Adam. The new word had enormous consequences; it implied an exalted condition before Adam disobeyed God, an implication which the biblical and early patristic word "transgression" (*parabasis*) did not have. Methodius also was the first to use the word "corruption" or "disintegration" (*thphora*) to describe the consequences of the fall on creation; he probably took the word from Romans 8:21.

Or, Cyril of Jerusalem (315–86), a bishop for many years, believed that children were sinless at birth, but with a hereditary bias toward sin. Human beings possessed the fullest possible freedom of choice. The remission of sins granted in adult baptism was for actual personal sins. There is no hint of the idea of original guilt in his writings.[48]

THE CAPPADOCIAN FATHERS

The province of Cappadocia (northeastern Turkey today) was served by three distinguished preachers and theologians in the last half of the fourth century, Basil the Great (330–79), Gregory of Nazianzus (330–89/90), and

46. Ibid., 196–97.
47. See Methodius, *From the Discourse on the Resurrection*, 3.1, Vol. 6.
48. See Willliams, *Ideas of the Fall*, 263.

his brother Gregory of Nyssa (335–94). They are best remembered for their rhetorical skills and vigorous defense of the theological formulation of the Council of Nicea. All three left an extensive legacy of writings—exegetical, theological, sermons.[49] What is rather surprising is that in this substantial body of literature they have very little to say about Genesis 3 and the sin of Adam and Eve. They are agreed that Adam's sin resulted in death, and that redemption is the rescue from the effects this sin. But they never define the mode of solidarity with Adam nor the nature of the sin which was transmitted. Gregory of Nazianzus and Gregory of Nyssa reflect considerable attraction to Origen, although both repudiate his idea of the pre-existence of souls and a pre-mundane fall. The two brothers tend to interpret Genesis 3 allegorically and to view Adam as equivalent to the human race rather than as an historical being.[50]

THE ANTIOCHENE SCHOOL

A final group of Greek fathers came from the School of Antioch in Syria, a theological school of thought which took a more Semitic and Hebraic approach to biblical interpretation than the more Hellenistic approaches of the Alexandrian school of Clement and Origen. The Antiochene School placed "an intensified emphasis" on individual responsibility.[51] The most prominent teachers of this school in the fourth century were John Chrysostom (b. ca. 350; d. 407) and Theodore of Mopsuestia (350–428). John Chrysostom from Antioch was an eloquent rhetorician, known as the "Golden Mouth," and a church reformer. He served for a short time as the bishop of Constantinople, but his fiery temperament and commitment to reform were ill suited to the context of the imperial capital. Chrysostom was in many respects the hermeneutical counter to Augustine's interpretation of Paul.[52] Theodore of Mopsuestia, also of Antioch, was a disciple of Chrysostom, and a monastic most of his life. Both men left a substantial body of writings–commentaries, theological works, and sermons. As with the Cappadocians, we find only occasional references to Genesis 3 or the

49. See Quasten, *Patrology*, Vol. 2, 203–93, for a listing and brief summary of their writings.

50. See Williams, *Ideas of the Fall*, 264–92; Tennant, *Sources*, 316–21, for summaries of the scattered references in the Cappadocian writings.

51. Kelly, *Early Christian Doctrines*, 373.

52. See Mitchell, *The Heavenly Triumphet*, especially 409–23, and Pagels, *Adam, Eve, and the Serpent*, 98–109, for comparisons and contrasts between Chrysostom and Augustine.

sin of Adam in the Garden. Chrysostom tended to minimize the consequences of Adam's sin to universal mortality. In his Homilies on Romans, Chyrsostom interpreted the critical phrase "for all sinned" in Romans 5:12 to mean "all became mortal."[53] He believed that infants were born without sin, and thus did not recognize any doctrine of inherited sinfulness.[54] Chrysostom also did not believe that man's freedom of will was limited by Adam's sin. Theodore of Mopsuestia viewed Adam as our type, but not as our ancestor. He agreed with Chrysostom that as a result of Adam's transgression, death passed to all human kind. Adam's sin resulted in a powerful bias (*hrope*) towards sin, but actual sins were not inevitable. Humans do not inherit the guilt of their parents' sins. Almost contemporaneous with Ambrosiaster and Augustine, Theodore interpreted the critical *eph ho* phrase in Romans 5:12 as "because of," not "in whom" as did Ambrosiaster and Augustine, and argued that each person received the sentence of death because of his/her own sin, not because of the sin of the first parents. He denied that baptism removed any kind of inherited sinfulness, but was administered as a pledge of future blessings.[55]

SUMMARY

The writings of the early theologians we have tracked so far represent the Greek-speaking eastern churches. All were agreed that sin entered the human race because of the transgression of Adam. Their understandings of Genesis 3 and of Adam's sin are quite similar and in many respects quite different from what we will find in the Latin-speaking western churches. The most critical point of difference between the East and the West is the absence among the Greek-speaking theologians of the concept of inherited guilt, which is the central point of the Latin doctrine of sin. Without exception among the Greek theologians, the inheritance from Adam's sin was mortality and corruption only. That is, the Greek fathers taught that humanity inherited Adam's punishment, death, but not Adam's sin. Guilt for sin could only be the result of a freely committed personal act. The Greek theologians consistently espoused the

53. "Homily x," *The Homilies of St. John Chrysostom on the Epistle of St. Paul the Apostle to the Romans*, Vol. 11.

54. See Tennant, *Sources*, 326; Kelly, *Early Christian Doctrines*, 349, citing *Matt Hom 28:3.*

55. See Kelly, *Early Christian Doctrines*, 373, citing Theodore *in Rom 5:12* and *in ps 50:7.*

sinlessness of infants as late as John Chrysostom and Theodore of Mopsuestia, contemporaries of Augustine.[56]

Other points of general agreement among the Greek-speaking theologians were: 1) a tendency to allegorize the Genesis 3 story or at least parts of it; 2) a tendency to conceive of Adam and Eve as childish, imperfect creatures at the time of their disobedience of God which thereby aborted their growth toward God's intended maturity for them; 3) the interpretation of the consequences of Adam and Eve's disobedience in terms of moral weakness and the loss of the assistance of the Holy Spirit, a deprivation or loss (*deprivatio*) rather than a fundamental corruption or deformity of human nature (*depravatio*); 4) the interpretation of the transmission of sin as social heredity–children being born outside of Paradise and being influenced by the example and instruction of their parents– rather than by biological heredity; 5) a strong emphasis on humanity's free will and personal responsibility; 6) the interpretation of the *eph ho* phrase in Romans 5:12 as "because of," not as "in whom;" 7) the explanation of evil as a result of the assaults of Satan and demons rather than any abstract idea of "original sin."*[57]

We are now through nearly 400 years of Christian church history and there is still no ontological understanding of sin. Sin is a result of freely committed acts which are nurtured by "the social heredity" in which people are born and live, and results in broken relationships, personal dysfunction and social chaos, and ultimately death. I am still looking for the basis for what I was taught in church and college.

* The early Greek Christian theological emphasis on free will and human accountability was a deliberate counter to the various forms of determinism and fatalism of much classical religion and philosophy from the time of Homer through the era of the Roman Empire. Belief in determinism was in direct conflict with the conviction of human responsibility that the followers of Jesus inherited from Judaism and which Jesus and his disciples reinforced with their calls for obedience as well as warnings of judgment from a just God.[58]

56. See Rondet, *Original Sin*, 108.

57. For similar summaries, see Blowers, "Original Sin," 839–40; Bray, "Original Sin," 37–43; Weaver, "Paul to Augustine," 187–88; Williams, *Ideas of the Fall*, 246–47.

58. See Pelikan, *The Christian Tradition*, Vol. 1, 279f; Weaver, "Anthropology," 60–65.

5

The Story of Original Sin in the Latin Church Fathers Prior to Augustine (200–400 CE)

T HE STORY OF SIN takes a different turn when we move from the Greek-speaking eastern churches to the Latin-speaking western churches in the early third century. The church fathers of the East represented a diversity of cultural, intellectual, and theological centers—Palestine, Syria, Asia Minor (Turkey today), Greece, Egypt, Gaul (France today)—and all read the Greek translation of the Old Testament (Septuagint) and the Greek New Testament writings. The Latin-speaking western church fathers in the "original sin" story came primarily from two centers, North Africa (Carthage and Hippo) and Italy (Milan and Rome), and some of the key thinkers read the critical biblical texts only in Latin translation rather than the original Greek.

TERTULLIAN (CA. 155–220)

The western story begins with Tertullian, a lawyer in Carthage, North Africa, who came from a pagan and military family. He became a Christian and was baptized late in the second century (ca. 198 CE), joined the Montanist sect within a decade (ca. 207), and left the "orthodox" wing of the church in 213 because of his Montanist convictions. Tertullian was a highly educated person in philosophy, law, and letters, especially in the Stoic school of thought. Next to Augustine he was the most important Latin theologian in the "story of original sin" during the patristic period.

Tertullian introduced a new anthropology which ultimately provided the framework for Augustine's theology of sin. Tertullian was "a thorough-going 'traducianist,'"[1] a teaching which he expounded in *A Treatise on the Soul [de anima]*,[2] a book written after his adoption of Montanism, a sect which the "orthodox" church declared heretical, but the book none-the-less exercised great influence in the "orthodox" church in the West. We are now introduced to the second theory of the origin of the soul. Origen believed in the pre-existence of the soul (theory # 1). Tertullian believed in the traducian origin of the soul (theory # 2), also called "generationism." According to this theory, the soul is material and parallels all the parts of the physical body, that is, it is "a duplicate body . . . a 'double' of the man";[3] the soul is *effigiata*.[4] The soul and the body are two separate substances which suffuse each other so subtly and completely that the human being is a single unity, dissolvable into its constituent parts only at death. In procreation a fragment of the father's soul shapes itself into a new soul bearing all the hereditary qualities of the father. The mother is entirely passive and receptive in the reproductive process and the creation of the new soul; heredity operates only through the father. Tertullian claimed that his anthropology was based on Scripture, specifically Genesis 1:27 and 2:7,[5] but he was in fact deeply, if not entirely, indebted to Stoic psychology, physiology, and ontology. Tertullian's materialist view of the soul was modified by Augustine who proposed that God created the soul of offspring by working on a spiritual substrate drawn from the soul of the generating male parent.[6] Though Tertullian did not develop this implication of his anthropology, later church fathers beginning with Ambrose, argued that a miraculous conception of Jesus was necessary in order to insure the sinlessness of his human nature by removing the male from his conception.

1. Kelly, *Early Christian Doctrines*, 175.

2. See *A Treatise on the Soul*, especially iii, iv, vi, xix, xxvii.

3. Rondet, *Original Sin*, 56.

4. Tertullian, *de anima* ix = *On the Soul* ix.

5. Ibid., iii.

6. See Augustine, *On the Soul and Its Origin*; Burns, "Traducianism," 1141; Kelly, *Early Christian Doctrines*, 175; Williams, *Ideas of the Fall*, 233–36. The third theory of the soul, "creationism," asserted that God created a soul for each body at the time of conception.

Tertullian's anthropology led directly to the theory of "seminal identity," according to which "all souls, actual or potential, were contained in Adam, since they must all be ultimately detached portions of the original soul breathed into him by God."[7] As Tertullian said, "every soul has been derived from Adam as its root"; it is a seed planted as an independent tree.[8] Or, "Every soul . . . by reason of its birth, has its nature in Adam until it is born again in Christ . . ."[9] "He teaches," asserts Rondet, "that every soul comes from Adam and bears the mark of the first sin. From the first moment of his existence man is affected by the original defect—*vitium originis*."[10] The Latin phrase *vitium originis*, "original moral fault" is introduced into the church's vocabulary for the first time by Tertullian. He thus articulates, says Tennant, "a realistic doctrine that Adam represented and summed up in himself the whole human race."[11] It is a short step from this anthropology to the doctrine of "original sin"; if all human souls are detached portions of the original soul which sinned, they must bear the moral responsibility for the primordial sin.

But it is not clear that Tertullian took that small but momentous step. His writings offer conflicting testimony. He also is a strong defender of human free will against various forms of determinism; for example, in *Against Marcion* and *Against Hermogenes* he repeatedly asserts that man is responsible for his choices and actions. Second, he has a very rich demonology which tends to blur the lines of his understanding of responsibility for Adam's sin.[12] Third, Tertullian objected to the practice of infant baptism. He reflects no knowledge of the theology of infant baptism as the way to cleanse from inherited sin. In fact, he was quite concerned about post-baptismal sin, and even argued against hurrying the end of the age of innocence.[13]

While it is not clear that Tertullian linked the hereditary bias towards evil derived from Adam's sin to the hereditary responsibility for Adam's sin which is the chief differentia of the Augustinian version of "original sin," it is evident that Tertullian was moving in the direction of a conception of "original guilt." He certainly argued for a much more severe doctrine of sin

7. Kelly, *Early Christian Doctrines*, 175.

8. *On the Soul*, xix.

9. Ibid., xl.

10. Rondet, *Original Sin*, 59–60.

11. Tennant, *Sources*, 332.

12. See *On the Soul*, iii; xxxix; xl; xli; *On Baptism*, v; *The Soul's Testimony*, iii.

13. See *On Baptism*, xviii.

than we have encountered so far regarding the hereditary consequences of Adam's sin, sin as corruption (*depravatio*) rather than weakness (*deprivatio*) as in the Greek fathers. In addition, he showed a strong tendency to view this corruption juridically or forensically, as though it were a crime, rather than medically, as though it were an illness. The conception of the inherited bias towards sin and the tendency to envisage sin under specifically legal categories, when combined with the theories of the "seminal identity" of Adam's descendants with Adam were laying the foundation for the idea of "original guilt." As the first writer to formulate a phrase for the "original moral fault" (*originis vitium*), Tertullian was moving the thinking of the church in the West toward Augustine's concept of "original sin" (*peccatum originale*).[14]

CYPRIAN (B. 200–210; D. 258 AS A MARTYR)

Cyprian was born into a wealthy and cultivated pagan family in Carthage, North Africa. Shortly following his conversion to Christianity, he became a priest and in late 248 or early 249 he was elected bishop of Carthage. Cyprian was a pastor whose theological thinking was profoundly shaped by Tertullian. An important part of his literary legacy are the numerous letters written to instruct and to edify. In one of these letters Cyprian makes the first explicit linkage between "original guilt" and the salvific effect of infant baptism. In a Letter written in behalf of a Council of 66 bishops in 253 CE to Fidus, an African bishop, who thought that baptism should be delayed until the eighth day on the analogy of Jewish circumcision, Cyprian urges that baptism be administered as soon after birth as possible:

> if, in the case of the greatest sinners and those sinning much against God, when afterward they believe, the remission of their sins is granted and no one is forbidden from baptism and of grace, how much more should an infant not to be prohibited, *who, recently born has not sinned at all, except that carnally born according to Adam, he has contracted the contagion of the first death from the first nativity*. He approaches more easily from this very fact to *receive the remission of sins because those which*

14. See Kelly, *Early Christian Doctrines*, 175–76; Rondet, *Original Sin*, 61; Williams, *Ideas of the Fall*, 241–45, for similar assessments.

> *are remitted* [in baptism] *are not his own sins but the sins of another.*[15]

Cyprian teaches a) that to be "carnally born" as a descendant of Adam involves participating in an hereditary infection by sin, and b) that the sin in question, which is forgiven ("remitted") by baptism, is not the new born's own, but the sin of another—that is, presumably, Adam's. Kelly believes that the biblical basis for Cyprian's linkage of the transmission of sin with the process of reproduction is Psalms 51:5, "Behold, I was conceived in iniquities, and in sins did my mother bear me," but there is no indication in Cyprian's letter that would support such a conclusion.[16]

AMBROSE (339–97)

Ambrose was an educated Roman aristocrat from a senatorial family very much at home in the halls of Roman power; he had been a provincial governor before unexpectedly being elected as the bishop of Milan in 374 while in the city to quell a riot. He was the person who baptized Augustine and was his most formative teacher in the church. Ambrose, therefore, is a very important figure in the "story of original sin."

As the bishop of Milan, Ambrose saw it as his duty to make clear to the Imperial court the uncompromising antithesis between the true Catholic Church and its many enemies. He taught and advocated, notes Peter Brown, "a world view marked by sharp antitheses and by hard boundaries. It was a harsh, defensive view of the world."[17] One part of this sharply defined worldview was a clear distinction between the church and the "spirit of the age" (*saeculum*), and the soul and the body. Ambrose was an ascetic, and believed that every human body bore one ugly scar, the scar of sexuality.[18] Augustine reports in his *Confessions* that the Bishop's teaching was so clear that he knew that if he were to accept baptism into the church by Ambrose it meant a commitment to sexual chastity.[19]

Ambrose was the first of the Latin fathers to explicitly teach the doctrine of the "Original Righteousness" or "Perfection" of Adam. He presented Adam in Paradise as a "heavenly being, exempt from the cares

---

15. Cyprian, "Letter 64," *Letters 1–81*, Vol. 51, 219; See also Kelly, *Early Christian Doctrines*, 176–77; Williams, *Ideas of the Fall*, 296. The italics are mine for emphasis.

16. See Kelly, *Early Christian Doctrines*, 176–77.

17. Brown, *The Body and Society*, 347.

18. Ambrose, *Expositio Lucan*, v.xxiv.

19. Augustine, *Confessions*, 8.11.27; 9.3.5.

and struggles of this life, endowed from the moment of his creation with the perfect balance of reason, will and appetite which fallen man lost."[20] Marriage and sexual intercourse were incompatible in this angelic state of existence. This doctrine of "Original Righteousness" is important because it maximized the "Fall-theory" by presenting the original state of man as one of unqualified perfection and bliss over against which Adam's sin is presented as a much more serious and inexcusable offense. This strong contrast was reflected in the shift in language used to describe Adam's disobedience; the tendency was to speak of Adam's "sin" as "fall" (*lapsus*) rather than "transgression" (*praevaricatio*), which literally means "walking crookedly" and is an almost exact translation of the Greek *parabasis*. Ambrose also introduced a quite new reason for the "fall": "Adam wanted to claim something which did not belong to him, that is, equality with the Creator."[21] The root cause of Adam's "fall" now became the sin of "pride,"[22] to which Ambrosiaster, a contemporary of Ambrose, added that Adam wanted to become like God.[23]

The definition of the root cause of Adam's sin as pride marked a significant shift from the eastern church. The locus of Adam's sin now was internal, not external (e.g., Satan) as in eastern church thought. Adam was now fully responsible for the "fall;" the Devil could no longer be blamed. The internalization of sin married to the concept of "hereditary sin" prepared the ground for Augustine's more radical theology.[24]

Ambrose talked about "hereditary sins" (*peccata hereditaria*) which are washed away by baptism and foot washing.[25] He makes numerous allusions and references to "original sin" as an inherited bias towards evil.[26] Many of these references are linked to a fear of sex. As a champion of virginity, Ambrose viewed sexual intercourse itself as sinful so that, in his view, humans are "born in" the sin of "our parents." This belief led Ambrose to the suggestion that the virgin birth of Christ was necessary in order to avoid the "physical pollutions" inherent in normal birth. "Hu-

20. Ambrose, *Expositio Psalmum*, cxviii, Serm. xv.36.

21. Ibid., cxviii.7–8.

22. See Ambrose, "Death as a Good," Vol. 65. "Death as a Good" was a sermon preached between 387 and 391.

23. Ambrosiaster, *Commentaries*, 5:14, 42. See also the discussion of Ambrosiaster's "Diabolical Tyranny" in Lunn-Rockliffe, *Ambrosiaster's Political Theology*, 146–74.

24. Bray, "Original Sin," 40–41.

25. Ambrose, *The Mysteries*, 31–32.

26. See Williams, *Ideas of the Fall*, 303, for a listing with references in Ambrose' writings.

man bodies, 'scarred' by sexuality," says Peter Brown, "could be redeemed only by a body whose virgin birth had been exempt from sexual desire."[27] Psalms 51:5 provided the biblical basis for this understanding.

Ambrose also took the momentous step that Tertullian did not; he explicitly linked Adam's sin with the inherited guilt of his posterity: "Assuredly we all sinned in the first man, and by the inheritance of his nature there has been transferred from that one man into all an inheritance of guilt. . . . So then Adam is in each one of us; for in him human nature itself sinned."[28] Or: "Adam existed, and in him we all existed. Adam perished, and in him all perished."[29] Or: "In Adam I fell, in Adam I was cast out of Paradise, in Adam I died; how shall the Lord call me back, unless He find me in Adam; guilty as I was in him, so now justified in Christ."[30]

Ambrose, late fourth century, for the first time explicitly articulates the theory of "seminal identity" in relationship to Adam's sin, "we all were in Adam and were Adam ." Therefore, when Adam "fell," all humanity "fell, or "sinned in him." The doctrine of "original sin" receives its first explicit formulation by Ambrose. As happens so often in the history of teacher-student relationships, the student, in this case, Augustine, will expand, enlarge, and dogmatize the initial formulation of the teacher. The sin of one man, Adam, will become the sin of universal humanity, and that theology will dominate the subsequent history of Western theology of sin as the "orthodox" theology.

Two other themes in Ambrose should be noted. First, the divinely appointed remedy for the hereditary disease of sinful human nature is baptismal regeneration as administered by the church. Secondly, contrary to all expectation, but still in agreement with his Greek predecessors, Ambrose insisted on the importance of free will or human responsibility, a freedom that will be lost with his student, Augustine.

27. Brown, *Body and Society*, 352.

28. Ambrose, *Apologia prophetae David*, lxxi.

29. Ambrose, *Expositio Lucan*, vii. 234.

30. Ambrose, *On the Death of Satyrus*, ii.6, vol. 10; and *On the Belief in the Resurrection*, ii.6, vol. 10.

AMBROSIASTER (ND)

Ambrosiaster, a contemporary of Ambrose, is a late fourth century commentator on Romans about whom we know almost nothing;[31] his commentary was sometimes incorrectly attributed to Ambrose or St. Hilarius. Gerald Bray, the recent translator of Ambrosiaster's commentaries on Romans and the Corinthian Letters, says "he was not a biblical scholar" and "his knowledge of Greek was rudimentary," and that "he made virtually no attempt to correct false or inadequate readings in the Latin version he was using by reference to the original language."[32] It is not clear which Latin version Ambrosiaster was using as the basis for his commentary on Romans. Scholars speculate that it may have been the *Itala*, which Augustine called "the best of the Latin versions circulating in his time," and "if so," says Bray, "we can only say that it provides clear evidence of the need for a fresh translation which Jerome was even then being commissioned to provide."[33] In addition, Bray asserts that "we have to admit that Ambrosiaster's interpretive skills are conditioned and sometimes constricted by a faulty text, leading him to conclusions that cannot be justified."[34] But by the end of the fourth century Ambrosiaster's commentary on Romans had become a standard work of Latin biblical study, and it retained its influence even after the publication of Jerome's Latin Vulgate translation in part because of its attribution to Ambrose.

Ambrosiaster's commentary played a significant role in Augustine's articulation of the doctrine of original sin. Ambrosiaster provided the crucial scriptural proof-text and exegesis for Augustine's theology, though based on a faulty translation of the Greek. Ambrosiaster's translation of Romans 5:12d is as follows: "*in whom all sinned.*" In the Commentary on

31. The commentary, which was written sometime between 366 and 384 in the city of Rome, is actually anonymous. For many years it was thought that the name Ambrosiaster was given by Erasmus, distinguished fifteenth- and sixteenth-century Renaissance scholar, because the commentary was attributed to Ambrose throughout the Middle Ages. Erasmus named the author Ambrosiaster because the author of the commentary "pretended to be St. Ambrose," according to Souter, *The Earliest Latin Commentaries*, 39. Ambrosiaster's commentary on Romans is part of a larger commentary on all the letters of Paul. Much of the ground work for *The Earliest Latin Commentaries* is found in Souter, *A Study of Ambrosiaster*. More recent research has established that the name was given by the Benedictines of St. Maur in their 1686–90 edition of Ambrose works, not by Erasmus. See Lunn-Rockliffe, *Ambrosiaster's Political Theology*, 31–32.

32. Ambrosiaster, "Translator's Introduction," *Commentaries*, xvi.

33. Ibid., xviii.

34. Ibid., xviii.

v. 12d he adds: "'in whom'" is "in the masculine gender (*in quo*) . . . his reference is to the universal race of man. . . . So then it is plain that all have sinned in Adam as in a lump (*quasi in massa*); for having been corrupted by sin himself, all those whom Adam fathered have been born under sin. For that reason we are all sinners, because we all descended from him."[35]

Augustine quoted this passage, mistranslation, mis-exegesis, and all. As nearly all modern Protestant and most Catholic commentators have pointed out, Ambrosiaster relied on a Latin version which rendered *eph ho* as *in quo*, "in whom," rather than as "on account of" or "because of."[36] Bray notes out that "Ambrosiaster clearly belongs to the Latin tradition and was only minimally influenced by Greek, Jewish and other sources."[37] Numerous historical theologians have pointed out that Ambrosiaster bequeathed to Western Christianity the supposed biblical foundation for its characteristic and "orthodox" theology of "original sin" and "original guilt" on the basis of a faulty reading of what Paul actually wrote.

What these historical theologians, however, have not for the most part told the church is that Ambrosiaster actually spoke about sin with two voices. Alexander Souter, one of the first twentieth century scholars to do a careful study of Ambrosiaster's writings, argues that Ambrosiaster's theology was "relatively nearer to Pelagius than to Augustine,"[38] which he adds "might be said of almost every Catholic writer," but before "the great Pelagian controversy."[39] Ambrosiaster, Souter asserts, had "not grasped the idea that before God man must always be the receiver and the favoured, never the giver or benefactor. Ambrosiaster, like many another, is obsessed by the idea that we can acquire merit with God, and the associated idea that certain labours on our part are necessary to gain it."[40] Furthermore, Ambrosiaster distinguished between the first and the second death. The second death represented eternal damnation for personal sins, but the good were free from this punishment. In addition, he personally denied the notion of inherited sin because the inheritance of sin is limited to the

---

35. Ambrosiaster, *Commentari Romanos*, v.12 [my translation]. See Ambrosiaster, *Commentaries*, 5.12, 40; Bray, *Romans*, 136; and Williams, *Ideas of the Fall*, 308, for similar translations.

36. See, for example, Bryan, *Preface to Romans*, 128–29; Cranfield, *Romans*, Vol. 1, 274–81; Fitzmyer, *Romans*, 405–17; Cranfield, "The Consecutive Meaning of EPH' HO in Romans 5:12," 321–39; Jewett, *Romans*, 375–76; Toews, *Romans*, 156–57, 399–400.

37. Ambrosiaster, "Translator's Introduction," *Commentaries*, xxi.

38. Souter, *Earliest Latin Commentaries*, 80.

39. Ibid., 64, 80.

40. Ibid., 80.

flesh; the soul is not inherited and thus "remains essentially unaffected by the corruption of human nature that dwells in the flesh."[41] Ambrosiaster also was not clear if humans had the power to refrain from sinning. He thus stood half-way between Pelagius, who asserted that humans had such power, and Augustine who denied such power to humans.

SUMMARY ON THE WESTERN STORY ON THE EVE OF AUGUSTINE

Church historian Gerald Bray of Beeson Divinity School asserted in 1994 that "it is virtually an axiom of historical theology that the doctrine of original sin . . . cannot be traced back beyond Augustine."[42] We have just noted that Bray is not quite correct. The theoretical and rhetorical foundations have been laid and articulated for Augustine by his predecessors in the western church.

From Tertullian forward the western fathers had a much more pessimistic anthropology, thanks, in part at least, to his linkage of the transmission of sin from Adam to his progeny through the traducian theory of the origin of the soul, and thus the concept of "seminal identity." Tertullian also introduced forensic categories for understanding sin as well as the important language of "original moral fault," *originis vitium*. Cyprian associated being "carnally born" with the "hereditary infection by sin" which needed the salvific washing of infant baptism. Ambrose transformed the unfallen Adam into a completely "Righteous" and "Perfect" "Superman" who "falls" in the Garden. He further linked Adam's sin with inherited guilt via the notion of the seminal identity with Adam's sin, and talked about "hereditary sins" (*peccata hereditaria*). Ambrosiaster added the critical exegetical proof-text with his mistranslation ["in whom, that is in Adam, all sinned"] and mis-exegesis ["it is plain that all have sinned in Adam as in a lump (*quasi in massa . . .*")] of Romans 5:12. All the pieces of the puzzle were on the table, and even loosely assembled. In fact, by 2009, following the translation of Ambrosiaster's *Commentary on Romans*, Bray says "it is fair to say that Ambrosiaster was an 'Augustinian' *avant la lettre*, and his commentary is important evidence that Augustine's ideas were more traditional and less innovative than is often thought."[43]

41. Ibid., 81–82. See also Ambrosiaster's comments on Romans 5.12–14, *Commentaries*, 40–43.

42. Bray, "Original Sin," 37.

43. Ambrosiaster, "Translator's Introduction," *Commetnaries*, xxi.

With one exception we have now left the theology of sin of the eastern church. Thanks to Tertullian and Cyprian, but especially to Ambrose and Ambrosiaster, sin has become ontological rather than relational. Sin is inherited. I am a sinner by nature, as I was taught in church and in college. So, what I was taught as a young person is grounded in the late fourth century Latin or western church teaching.

The one hold-over of eastern thought, the exception I just mentioned, is that all of the western fathers to this point still believed in human free will and responsibility. How they could hold together the determinism of ontological sin and human responsibility is a puzzle, which Augustine realized early. The notion of human free will regarding sin disappeared as soon as Augustine put together the pieces of the puzzle placed on the table by his predecessors. Augustine's theology of original sin had no room for human free will.

Even if we are generous with the early Bray's understandings of historical theologians, they have kept the secret from most biblical scholars, theologians, and pastors, at least within the evangelical world. The doctrine of "original sin" seems well and very much alive in most Christian churches, although one detects restlessness around the edges.

But it is worth observing that none of the writers reviewed so far, all major pastor-bishops-theologians in the early church through the first four centuries, asserts that the "doctrine of original sin" belongs to the essence of the gospel or "the Deposit of the Faith." No mention is made of the doctrine either in the rules of faith, in the local baptismal creeds of the period, or in the ecumenical Councils of Nicaea (325), First Council of Constantinople (381), Ephesus (431), and Chalcedon (451) that were shaping the foundational theological convictions of the post-Constantinian church.[44] The doctrine does not appear in a creed of the church until the Council of Orange (529) and that because of the influence of Augustine.

44. See the magisterial study of the early creeds by Pelikan and Hotchkins, *Creeds and Confessions*, Vol. 1, 37–181.

6

Augustine's Theology of Original Sin (354–430)

AUGUSTINE WAS BORN IN a small town in North Africa (Thagaste, Souk-Ahras in north-east Algeria today) in 354 to a pagan father and very devout Christian mother. Following an education in the liberal arts, especially Latin literature, in preparation for teaching, Augustine associated himself with a Manichean ascetic community despite the fact that he was living with a low class concubine by whom he had a son. Short teaching stints in Carthage and Rome led to a teaching position in Milan, the residence of the western emperor Valentinian II and Ambrose, the Bishop of Milan. Augustine converted to Christianity in 386 through the influence of Ambrose' preaching, but not before he sent his concubine of 16 years and his son back to North Africa. He was baptized into the Catholic Church on Easter Eve 387 by Ambrose. In 388 Augustine returned to his family house in Thagaste with some friends in order to establish a monastic community that would focus on the study of the Bible and Neoplatonic philosophy. On a visit to Hippo in 391 he was mobbed and forced to be ordained a priest. Five years later he was ordained as Bishop to replace the elderly Valerius in Hippo as the Primate of Numidia, a large province in North Africa.

Augustine was first and foremost a preacher and polemicist; he was not a scholar.[1] He, for example, did not read the original biblical lan-

---

1. See Bonner, *Augustine*; Brown, *Augustine*; and O'Donnell, *Augustine*, for excellent biographies of Augustine.

guages, Hebrew or Greek, and so was dependent for his interpretation of the critical biblical texts that he used in arguments with his opponents on the "clumsy"[2] Latin translations of other people, even on mistranslations. Augustine's primary opponents in his polemical writings were first the Manicheians in the earlier part of his life and then the Donatists and Pelagians in his mature and later years.

EARLY FORMULATION

Augustine's initial formulation of the doctrine of the "original sin" was in reaction to the Manicheian movement of which he had been a novitiate for nearly ten years. In 394–95, seven or eight years after his baptism in Milan, Augustine responded to a Manichaean opponent or question in a discussion of Romans 9:20 with these words: "we have all become one lump of clay, i.e., a lump of sin . . . we as sinners deserve nothing other than eternal damnation."[3] A few years later in a book written in 397 from Hippo to Simplician, successor to Ambrose in Milan, Augustine in a discussion of Romans 7:7–25 wrote that sin originated in the transgression of Adam and became ingrained in human nature through its transmission by physical heredity.[4] Augustine in this book uses the epoch-making phrase "original sin" (*originale peccatum*) for the first time in the history of Christian thought.[5] The phrase defines a sinful quality which is inherent in human nature, albeit involuntarily acquired. It is considered by Augustine to be sin in the fullest sense of the term; it involves guilt and it deserves punishment.[6] A little later he uses the term "original guilt" (*originalis reatus*).[7] The critical terms that will define Augustine's mature doctrine of "original sin," *originale peccatum* and *originalis reatus*, are used in 397. In the same book Augustine again asserts that the human stock constitutes a single "lump of sin" (*massa peccati*): "all men are a mass of sin, since, as the apostle says, 'in Adam all die' (I Cor. 15:22), and to Adam the entire human race

---

2. Fredriksen's characterization in *Sin*, 113.

3. See, Question 68, 3, *Eighty-Three Different Questions*, Vol. 70. The "lump of sin" phrase is the translation of *massa peccati*, the problematic phrase suggested by Ambrosiaster.

4. "First Question: Romans 7:7–25, 4," *To Simplician—On Various Questions. Book I.*

5. Ibid., 10, 11.

6. Ibid., 11.

7. Ibid., 20.

traces the origin of its sin against God."[8] The human race, Augustine goes on, is justly doomed to everlasting death.[9] Out of this "lump of sin" God in mercy selected a fixed number of souls who through no merits of their own were brought to baptism, justified and saved. The rest of humankind is left by God's justice in the "lump of sin" on its way to judgment in the bottomless pit.[10]

Williams in his Brampton Lectures argues that the theology of sin Augustine articulates so soon after his conversion to Christianity embodies some of the worst "features of North African Christianity in a peculiarly concentrated form."[11] The harshness of life under the African desert sun had profoundly shaped the theological world views of Tertullian and Cyprian. Through their influence there had developed a legalistic and pitiless Latin-Punic theology. Traditional Christian thought in North Africa was narrowly defined with a predominantly forensic conception of sin and a quasi-commercial treatment of merit. It also reflected an indifference to those outside of these boundaries (e.g., the various controversies over the purity of the church in North Africa). This theology had a profound influence on Augustine. It was fertile ground, according to Williams, for Augustine's notions of "seminal identity," "original guilt," and the "lump of sin" (*massa peccati*).

The theology of "original sin" that Augustine articulated in 397 to Simplician is reflected clearly and repeatedly in Augustine's most famous writing, his *Confessions*,[12] which he began to write at the same time, shortly after he became bishop of Hippo. Augustine confesses to God that he was never innocent, not even at the moment of his birth (I, vii). His infant sins were real sins with real guilt which he inherited from his parents even if he could not remember them. Not only Augustine, but all humankind were "sons of Adam" (I, ix) and "sons of Eve" (I, xvi). Sin dwells in him due to the voluntary sin of Adam "because I am a son of Adam" (VIII, x). Augustine inherited this sin from his parents by means of reproductive generation (I, vii). Adam is the origin of sin, and the sins that "flowed out of his loins" are the cause of universal humanity's sins (XIII, xx).[13]

8. "Second Question: Romans 9:10–29, 16," Ibid.

9. Ibid.

10. Ibid., 16, 17.

11. Williams, *Ideas of the Fall*, 330.

12. *Loeb Classical Library*. References are in brackets in the text. See O'Donnell, *Augustine*, 35–86, for the contextualization and a helpful interpretation of the *Confessions*.

13. See Rigby, *Original Sin*, for a very helpful analysis of Augustine's theology of

THE REACTION TO PELAGIUS

By the turn of the end of the fourth and the beginning of the fifth centuries, the classical language of Augustine's doctrine of "original sin" was in place. It was a theology, according to Paul Rigby, deeply rooted in Augustine's own experience as narrated in the *Confessions*.[14] This early formulation became fixed and dogmatic in Augustine's reaction to the teachings of Pelagius and his followers in a movement known as Pelagianism.[15] That controversy began in 411 and lasted for twenty years. Pelagius was an ascetic and moralistic monk from Britain or Ireland. He came to Rome in the 380s following extensive travels in the eastern parts of the Roman Empire where he was influenced by the more positive view of human nature in the eastern Christian theological tradition. Central to his theology was the belief in human free will and responsibility. God created humans with the ability to choose life or death, and asked them to choose life. Pelagius believed that each soul was created by God at the time of conception ("creationism") and thus could not come into the world tainted by original sin transmitted from Adam. The assumption that human beings were born with a bias toward sin was an insult to God, according to Pelagius. Adam's sin did have disastrous consequences for humanity; it introduced death and the habit of disobedience. But the latter was propagated by example, not by physical descent. Infant baptism, Pelagius proposed, was benedictory, not salvific for the remission of sins. He also rejected any notion of God's advanced predestination of some people for salvation; God's predestination operated only in accordance with the quality of the lives people lived.[16]

While in Rome Pelagius encountered Ambrosiaster's *Commentary on Romans* and wrote his own commentaries on the Epistles of Paul between 405/6 and 410. In his exposition of Romans 5:12 Pelagius denied the hereditary transmission of sin. He interpreted Paul to be speaking of social inheritance in Romans 5:12; humans sin by voluntary imitation

---

original sin in the *Confessions*.

14. Ibid., 2.

15. See McWilliams, "Pelagius, Pelagianism," 887–90, for a good introduction and bibliography to Pelagius and Pelagianism.

16. See Brown, *Augustine*, 340–52; Kelly, *Early Christian Doctrines*, 357–61; McWilliams, "Pelagius," 887–90; Pagels, *Adam*, 127–50; Pelikan, *Christian Tradition*, 313–16; Weaver, "Paul to Augustine," 199–204; Williams, *Ideas of the Fall*, 332–38, for more extensive summaries of Pelagius' teachings.

of Adam's sin, never by a fault inherent in human nature.[17] In addition, Pelagius argued on the basis of Romans 5:15 that righteousness had more power to make alive than sin had to put to death, and that the righteousness of Christ benefitted even those who did not believe. He also made the case that if baptism cleansed inherited sin, the children of two baptized persons could not inherit sin because the parents could not transmit a sin which they did not possess.[18]

By the end of the first decade of the fifth century the Latin speaking western church had two different theologies that had been articulated quite independently of each other. The essential shape of Augustine's doctrine of sin was developed from Hippo in 397 in response to questions from Simplician in Milan and in his own *Confessions*, also written in Hippo, before Augustine ever heard of Pelagius. Pelagius in Rome outlined a quite different theology that agreed at critical points with the Greek tradition of human free will and responsibility, which Ambrose in Milan and Ambrosiaster in Rome also had taught. But, Pelagius unequivocally rejected Ambrosiaster's interpretation of Romans 5:12 regarding the transmission of sin through Adam and the seminal identity of all humanity in Adam's sin.

THE ROLE OF INFANT BAPTISM

As the distinguished church historian Jaroslav Pelikan states, "if the touchstone of orthodoxy was adherence to the true faith concerning the Trinity and the person of Christ," it was incorrect to call the teachings of Pelagius a heresy.[19] But two things happened to change the dynamics. First, Pelagius and his companions left Rome for North Africa in 410/11. Pelagius stayed in North Africa only briefly before proceeding to Palestine. However, two of his followers, Celestius and Julian of Eclanum (near Benevento in south Italy), took up Pelagius' cause. Julian, an aggressive polemicist in his own right, became the "architect of 'the Pelagian dogma'" and was "the last and probably the most formidable of all the antagonists with whom Augustine crossed swords in a lifetime

17. See *Pelagius' Commentary on St. Paul's Epistle to the Romans*; Souter, *Pelagius' Expositions*, Vol. I, Vol. II.

18. See Souter, *Earliest Latin Commentaries*, 219, for a discussion of Pelagius' exposition of Romans 5:15.

19. Pelikan, *Christian Tradition*, 316.

of polemical writing."[20] Augustine, ever the polemicist, could not resist a good fight. Second, the presenting issue now became infant baptism. Again, as Pelikan points out, "the standard of trinitarian orthodoxy, the Nicene Creed, contained the statement: 'We confess [in the Latin text: 'I confess'] one baptism for the forgiveness of sins.'"[21] The intent of the phrase "one baptism" in 325 (the date of the Nicean Creed) was to disallow the possibility of rebaptism, and the phrase "remission of sins" was composed regarding adult candidates, not the status of infants and children.[22] But by the early fifth century the meaning of the baptismal language had changed; it now referred to the baptism of infants. Augustine argued for a literal understanding of the creedal statement, "one baptism for the remission of sin." Augustine insisted that only his doctrine of original sin did justice to the church's practice of infant baptism. Pelikan again: "the Augustinian theory provided a theological justification for an unchallengeable sacramental practice. The doctrine of original sin, of the fall, of the transmission of sin, and of the necessity of grace appeared to make sense of infant baptism . . ."[23] The battle was joined. But, remember, what I am summarizing in a few paragraphs, represented a twenty-year conflict in the western church, especially in North Africa, and was argued in many different writings and sermons by Augustine.

THE CENTER OF AUGUSTINE'S DOCTRINE OF ORIGINAL SIN

Augustine's argument for "original sin" begins with a portrayal of the "unfallen" Adam as a "righteous" and "perfect" man; that is, Augustine accepts Ambrose' doctrine of the "original righteousness" and "perfection" of Adam in Paradise. He was the perfect physical human being—no physical defects, no health problems, no illnesses, no effects of aging, endowed with immortal youth. Adam was an intellectual genius; his mental powers were far superior to those of the most brilliant philosophers and scientists of Augustine's time—he could give appropriate names to all the animals

---

20. Bonner, *Augustine*, 344.

21. Pelikan, *Christian Tradition*, 316.

22. So Weaver, "Paul to Augustine," 202.

23. Pelikan, *Christian Tradition*, 317–18. For repeated discussions of the relation of Augustine's doctrine of original sin and infant baptism see Ferguson, *Baptism in Early Church*, especially 627–33, 803–16, 856–57. See also Wright, "Augustine and Baptism," 287–310.

in the world. His moral character was without flaw. He had the moral capacity not to sin, *posse non peccare*. Adam's free-will was the absolute sovereign of his being, exercising complete control over all elements of his appetites and feelings. The sexual appetite in particular was entirely subject to the control of his will. If Adam had remained in Paradise he and Eve would have had children, but under the full control of reason, that is, without any sexual passion. Adam in Paradise knew no struggle. He had no temptations.[24]

Adam's sin or "the Fall" was a sin of the will. The "righteous" and "perfect" unfallen Adam made a choice, and he sinned, he fell. Adam's sin was not due to concupiscence because it hardly existed in unfallen man, nor to appetite or some other weakness, but to a direct and wilful transgression of the command of God, and as such included in itself all possible forms of sin. Adam's choice was so serious, because, following Ambrose, Augustine believed Adam sinned due to pride because he wanted to be like God which was the greatest of all blasphemies.[25] Augustine himself defines the comprehensive nature of Adam's sin in these words: it involved the sin of

> pride, since man chose to be under his own dominion rather than under God's; also blasphemy, since man refused to believe God; and murder, for he rushed headlong into death; and spiritual fornication, since the innocence of the human soul was corrupted by the seduction of the serpent; and theft, since man appropriated to himself forbidden food; and avarice, since he craved for more than sufficed for his needs; and whatever else may be found diligent reflection to have been involved in the commission of this one sin.[26]

And Adam's choice fundamentally changed human nature and condemned universal humanity because Adam's sin "passed unto all men"; it is original sin [*peccatum originale*] or transmitted sin [*peccatum ex traduce*].

---

24. See Augustine, *The Literal Meaning of Genesis*, 18, 32; *City of God*, xii, xxii; xiii, i, xxii; xiv, x; *Marriage and Desire*, i, i, vi, vii, viii; *Unfinished Work Against Julian*, 5.61; see also Brown, *Body and Society*, 387–407; Fredriksen, *Sin*, 120–21; Rondet, *Original Sin*, 120; Williams, *Ideas of the Fall*, 362.

25. Augustine, *Literal Meaning of Genesis*, 5; *City of God*, xiv, xiii; *Faith, Hope, and Charity* (also known as *Enchiridion*), Vol. 3, 28; *Answer to Julian*, ii, 5.17; see also Bray, "Original Sin," 45; Rondet, *Original Sin*, 120.

26. Augustine, *Faith, Hope, and Charity*, 45; see also *Literal Meaning of Genesis*, 11, and *City of God*, xiv.xiii on pride as the fundamental sin; and Mann, "Augustine on evil and original sin," 40–48.

Augustine makes that point repeatedly. He made it in 397 to Simplician and he makes it repeatedly in his conflict with the Pelagians.

The Literal Meaning of Genesis, written between 401 and 415: "Infants must be baptized because its soul was 'contaminated' from the first soul of Adam who sinned. For it was not by any sin but rather by nature that it was so made . . ."[27]

The Forgiveness of Sins and the Baptism of Little Ones, the first work written against the Pelagians in the late fall of 411 or early in 412: "Paul said, 'Through one man sin entered the world, and through sin death' (Rom 5:12). This means by propagation, not imitation; otherwise, he would say, 'through the devil.' He is speaking of the first man, who was called Adam, a point which no one doubts. And 'thus,' he said, 'it was passed on to all human beings' (Rom. 5:12)."[28]

> Then, note, the carefulness, the propriety, the clarity with which the next clause is stated, 'in whom all sinned' (Rom 5:12). For if you have here understood the sin that entered the world through the one man in which sin all have sinned, it is certainly clear that personal sins of each person by which they alone sinned are distinct from this one in which all have sinned, when all were that one man. But if you have understood, not the sin, but the one man, in which one man all have sinned, what could be clearer than that clear statement?[29]

City of God, written between 413–26, that is, through the heat of the Pelagian controversy:

> The first sinners, received punishment by death on such terms that whatever should spring from their stock was also to be held liable to the same penalty; for they were to have no progeny other than that which resembled them. Their punishment, in fact, was commensurate with the enormity of their guilt and *effected in their original nature a change for the worse*. As a result, what came initially as punishment to the first human beings who sinned also follows as a natural consequence in the rest who are born [xiii, iii. Italics for emphasis are mine].
>
> Man the offspring is just the same thing as the parent. Therefore the entire human race that was to pass through woman into offspring was contained in the first man when that conjugal couple received the divine sentence condemning them to

27. *Literal Meaning of Genesis*, 15.

28. In *Answer to the Pelagians*, 9.10.

29. Ibid., 10.11.

punishment, and man reproduced what man became, not when he was being created, but when he was sinning and being punished . . . [xiii, iii].

Augustine's response to Irenaeus and the Greek fathers is stated clearly:

> For the first man was not reduced by sin or punishment to an infantile state of mental dullness and bodily weakness, such as we see in small children . . .

> . . . *his human nature was so corrupted and changed within him* that he suffered in his members a rebellious disobedience of desire, was bound by the necessity of dying and thus reproduced what he himself had come to be . . . that is offspring liable to sin and death [xiii, iii—italics for emphasis are mine].

> *We were all in that one man* since all of us were that one man who fell into sin through the woman who was made from him before sin. We did not yet have individually created and apportioned shapes in which to live as individuals; *what already existed was the seminal substance from which we were generated. Obviously, when this substance was debased through sin . . . no man could be born in any other condition.* Thus from the abuse of free will has come the linked sequence of our disaster by which the human race is conduced through an uninterrupted succession of miseries from that original depravity . . . [xiii, xiv—italics for emphasis are mine].

Faith, Hope, and Charity, written between 420 and 423:

> Children are involved not only in the sin of our first parents but also in the sins of their own parents. That is what the divine sentence means: "I shall visit the iniquities of the fathers upon their children."[30]

> We are born in sin as Psalm 50:7 explains: "I was conceived in iniquities; and in iniquities did my mother nourish me in her womb." Nor did he say, as he might have done correctly, "in iniquity" and "in sin"; but he chose to say "iniquities" and "sins," because in that one sin which passed on to all men and which was so great that by it *human nature was changed* and subjected to the necessity of dying, and many more sins . . .[31]

30. *Faith, Hope and Charity,* 46, citing Deut 5:9.
31. Ibid., 46. Italics are mind for emphasis.

The change of human nature effected by Adam's sin is so fundamental that the washing and cleansing of baptism does nothing to change the human nature of the parents and thus benefit the children born to regenerate parents. Thus Augustine in 418: "The fault of our nature remains in our offspring so deeply impressed as to make it guilty, even when the guilt of the self-same fault has been washed away in the parent by the remission of sins."[32]

TWO CRITICAL METAPHORS

Augustine in his numerous writings uses two metaphors to explain the nature of the transmitted sin, one is medical, *vitium*, and second is legal, *reatus*. The medical metaphor, *vitium*, means that humanity suffers from a hereditary moral disability, first acquired by Adam and since transmitted from generation to generation. The moral disease consists in the uncontrollable tyranny of sexual passion (concupiscence) over human beings. Concupiscence is the tendency which drives human beings to turn from the supreme and unchangeable God to find satisfaction in the changeable, that is, in creatures. This drive is involuntary even in the best of humanity, and finds its expression most clearly in the sexual drive. There is a real sense in which for Augustine concupiscence refers primarily to sexual lust. Thus many interpreters of Augustine have suggested that original sin as vitium equals concupiscence which equals sexual passion. Others are less certain about that equation.[33] At any rate, the act of reproduction inevitably stains every child with original sin so that everyone is literally "born in sin," that is, in the sin of the parents. Therefore, Augustine agrees with Ambrose that it was necessary for Christ to be born free from sex. Thus, "the soul of Christ was not generated from the original human soul. . . . Christ . . . assumed the visible substance of the flesh from the flesh of the Virgin; the formative principle of His conception, however, was not from the seed of a man, but it came from above in a far different way."[34]

The corruption of human nature due to *vitium* for Augustine meant the loss of free will. The power of the human will was irreparably weakened by the fall; human beings are no longer able to make choices which are not tainted by sin. But Augustine did not draw the logical conclusion

---

32 *A Treatise on the Grace of Christ, and on Original Sin,* Book II, 44.

33. See the discussion in De Simone, "Modern Research," 214–17.

34. *Literal Meaning of Genesis,* 20; see also the discussion in Brown, *Body and Society,* 407.

of this interpretation which Calvin did, the "total depravity" of the human will and thus of human beings.

The legal or forensic metaphor, *reatus*, asserts that humanity is subject to the inherited legal liability for Adam's sin, and therefore, to judicial punishment for his sin. The transfer of original guilt from Adam to his posterity is explained via the theory of seminal identity—when Adam sinned he included within himself, in a strictly physiological sense, the whole human race, everyone who proceeded from his genitals. Adam was the universal human nature, and as such subsumed in himself all the particular human beings who have been born since. Consequently, all humans sinned "in Adam," in the sense that at the moment of "the Fall" they were all infinitesimally minute portions of the Adam who sinned. The biblical basis for Augustine's use of the theory of seminal identity was the Hebrew 7:9–10 text which reports that Levi was in the loins of Abraham when the latter paid tithes to Melchizedek; the author of Hebrews is interpreted to have assumed that Levi shared seminally in the payment of those tithes.[35] It follows, according to Augustine, that all humans are subject to the penalty of eternal hell for a sin they committed pre-natally in Adam's genitals.[36]

Much of Augustine's theology of original sin was framed while he believed in some form of the traducian theory of the origin of the soul.[37] That theory facilitated his belief in "seminal identity." Furthermore, according to Bonner, the theory of "seminal identity" was "fully in keeping with the temperament of African Christianity, with its fierce and rather pessimistic biblical strain," and on the intellectual level harmonized "with a tendency in western Pauline exegesis, expressed in the writings of Ambrosiaster."[38] But by the early fifth century traducianism was under heavy criticism in philosophical and theological circles. When he wrote *The Literal Meaning of Genesis* (401–15) he claims to be undecided between traducianism and creationism [Book 10]. But it really does not make much difference because biological reproduction is the means for the transmission of sin.[39]

35. Augustine, *Literal Meaning of Genesis*, 20; *Against Julian*, i, 48.

36. See Augustine, *City of God*, xiii.xiv; *Faith, Hope, and Charity*, xxvi, xxvii.

37. See Fredriksen, "Body and Soul," 108–9; Rist, *Augustine*, 317–18.

38. Bonner, "Augustine on Romans 5:12," 245.

39. Weaver, "Paul to Augustine," 203–4.

THE BIBLICAL BASIS

The critical biblical text Augustine used for his doctrine of original sin was Romans 5:12 as translated and interpreted by Ambrosiaster. Augustine cites this text more than 150 times, overwhelmingly in his anti-Pelagian writings, according to Bonner.[40] The numerous citations of Ambrosiaster's translation and interpretation, asserts Bonner, "illustrates the complete confidence Augustine had both in the translation . . . and in his own understanding of the verse as a whole."[41] The other texts which he cited are Job 24:4, 5 [from a faulty Latin translation of the LXX], Psalms 51:5; John 3:5; Ephesians 2:3.

Augustine was not unaware of the problematic of his use of Ambrosiaster's translation and interpretation of the Romans 5:12 text. Julian of Eclanum, Augustine's chief protagonist knew Greek and also had access to a correct text, was severely critical of Ambrosiaster's translation and Augustine's use of it. Augustine defended his interpretation repeatedly,[42] including the use of Ambrosiaster's commentary and citations from Ambrose's commentary on Luke.[43] It is Bonner's belief that Augustine never considered the possibility that the Greek original might be susceptible to any interpretation other than Ambrosiaster's.[44] Bonner goes on to assert that "it is certainly unlikely that Augustine would have changed his doctrine even if he had discovered that it was not supported by the actual words of St. Paul."[45]

Augustine believed that his doctrine of original sin was supported by the tradition of the church. But it is hard to find much support for Augustine's theology beyond Ambrose, whose commentary on Luke he cites often,[46] and Ambrosiaster. They put the pieces of the puzzle on the table, but no one put the puzzle together until Augustine did in his response to Simplician in 397 and in his battle with the Pelagians from 411 onwards.

---

40. Bonner, "Augustine on Romans 5.12," 242. See also Bonaiuti, "Genesis of Augustine's Idea of Original Sin," 159–75, for an argument for Augustine's direct dependence on Ambrosiaster.

41. Bonner, "Augustine on Romans 5.12," 242.

42. See, for example, *Answer to Julian*, 6.75; *Unfinished Work Against Julian*, 2.48–55; *Faith, Hope, and Love*, 45, 47; *On Nature and Grace*, 48; and *Letters*, Vol. 3, 157; *Letters*, Vol. 4, 176.

43. See Weaver, "Paul to Augustine," 202–3.

44. Bonner, "Augustine on Romans 5.12," 247.

45. Ibid., 247.

46. See Rondet, *Original Sin*, 130, note 44 for a detailed listing.

SUMMARY

Augustine in his initial response to a question from Simplician in 397 introduced the words "original sin" (*originale peccatum*), "original guilt" (*originale reatus*) and "lump of sin" (*messa peccati*), and for the rest of his life consistently taught that sin originated in the transgression of Adam and was transmitted from generation to generation through human reproduction. A historic and cataclysmic event occurred in the Garden of Eden—a "Righteous" and "Perfect" Adam in Paradise wilfully chose to disobey God because of pride and fundamentally changed human nature through his action. That "original sin" as "moral disability" (*vitium*) and as "legal liability" (*reatus*) was passed on genetically from Adam to all subsequent human beings because all human beings were present in Adam's semen. All human beings subsequent to Adam, except for the few elect to salvation by God's grace and mercy, were condemned to eternal hell for a sin they committed pre-natally in Adam's genitals. The biblical basis for Augustine theology of original sin was a mistranslation and mis-exegesis of Romans 5:12.

A CRITICAL EXAMINATION OF THE AUGUSTINIAN THEOLOGY OF ORIGINAL SIN

The picture of the "Righteous" and "Perfect" Adam in Paradise is without biblical foundation and without historical tradition in the church until Ambrose. There is no "Perfect Man" in the Genesis narrative of the creation of Adam and Eve, nor in the New Testament writings, nor in the Jewish or Greek and early Latin Christian interpretations of the Genesis stories of human creation and disobedience. Ambrose in the late fourth century introduces a mythology which Augustine uses as the foundation to construct his theology of original sin.

The biblical basis for Augustine's theology of original sin also is without foundation. Augustine grounds his theology in five biblical texts: Job 24:4–5 [faulty Latin translation from the LXX] [25:4–5 NRSV]; Psalm 51:5; John 3:5; Ephesians 2:5; Romans 5:12. Two of the proof-texts are based on mistranslations (Job and Romans), the use of the Ephesians texts is "specious," according to Rondet, and neither the Psalms nor the John texts support Augustine's idea of "original sin."[47] The critical text for Augustine was Romans 5:12, and "the Greek does not and cannot bear the

47. See Rondet, *Original Sin*, 128; see also Williams, *Ideas of the Fall*, 379.

interpretation which Augustine wished to place upon it."[48] Rondet, a Catholic theologian greatly indebted to Augustine's theology, admits Augustine was an "unreliable exegete with regard to details,"[49] but his theology of sin became official orthodox church dogma in the Council of Orange in 529, and is repeated in many Christian creeds and confessions of faith (e.g., Lutheran: Augsburg, 1530; Roman Catholic: Council of Trent, 1563–64; Reformed: Second Helvetic Confession, 1566; Westminster Confession, 1646; Anglican: Thirty-Nine Articles, 1563; Methodism: Articles of Religion, 1784) despite the fact that it was based on a wrong translation of the text and on faulty exegesis of the text.[50] And that in direct opposition to the many ancient orthodox Christians and Pelagian opponents of Augustine who knew the Greek and translated the critical phrase in Romans 5:12 as "because all sinned" rather than as "in whom [that is, in Adam] all sinned."

Bonner, one of the biographers of Augustine, asks why did Augustine not re-think his position when confronted with people who read the Greek?" Bonner's hypothesis is that "Augustine was so absorbed by his theory that he did not give it the critical examination which it required."[51]

The theory of "seminal identity" again is without biblical basis. It is grounded entirely in debates within Greco-Roman philosophy, especially Stoicism, about the origin of the soul. The traducian theory of the origin of the soul was already in disfavor in Augustine's time. He had to defend it. Augustine's doubts about traducianism and possible switch to a creationist theory of the origin of the soul is of little help. Because he then had to answer the question of how a good God could create so many pure, sinless souls and place them into bodies corrupted by original sin through sexual passion and so damn them to eternal punishment. Augustine responded to this problem by an appeal to God's "occult justice:" "by how much divine justice is loftier than human justice, by so much it is inscrutable and by so much it differs from human justice. . . . Think on these thing, and forbear to set God the Judge in comparison with human judges, that God whom we must not doubt to be just even when he does what seems to men unjust, or what, if it were done by men, would actually be unjust."[52]

---

48. Bonner, *Augustine*, 372.

49. Rondet, *Original Sin*, 219.

50. See Pelikan and Hotchkis, *Creeds and Confessions*, and Leith, *Creeds of the Church*, for many more creedal and confessional statements.

51. Bonner, *Augustine*, 372.

52. *Unfinished Work against Julian*, 3.24; see also Weaver, "Paul to Augustine," 203; and Williams, *Ideas of the Fall*, 381.

It is clear that Augustine's contemporaries and critics knew that there was no justice in making humans responsible before a Just God for an act they did not commit. And it is clear that Augustine knew that too; any time one appeals to the mysterious justice of God to defend a weak argument, one has conceded the argument.

This evaluation of Augustine is a sad one. His *Propositions from the Epistle to the Romans: Unfinished Commentary on the Epistle to the Romans*, written in the mid-390s before any engagement with Pelagianism, indicates that Augustine knew that Paul wrote Romans to address the question of whether the gospel came to the Jews alone because of their works of Law or to all the nations through faith in Christ.[53] But the potential that this insight gave Augustine for a historical and contextual reading of Paul got lost between the early Augustine and the Augustine of *ad Simplicanum* and then the later controversy with Pelagianism. Paul's theology of sin that equalizes relations between Jews and Gentiles so that "the righteousness of God" could be revealed in Messiah Jesus equally to Jews and Gentiles disappeared as Romans, especially one text in Romans, became a quarry to incorrectly legitimate a doctrine of original sin that universalized Adam's sin and damned all humanity since Adam, except a small number of elect.

ASSESSMENT

By the time we get to Augustine in the fifth century CE in our story, ten to fifteen centuries from the story of Genesis 3 (depending on the dating of Genesis), we are a long way from the beginning in Genesis 3, from the interpretation of Paul in Romans, and from the infant or child-like Adam of the Greek fathers. The Genesis 3 story turns out to be a marginal one in the Hebrew scriptures; it is never cited or retold to explain the origin of sin or to talk about "the fall." In fact, the Hebrew Scriptures do not assume a "fall." Deuteronomy 30:11–14 is more characteristic in its assumption that humankind can obey the purposes of God.

Paul holds Adam accountable for releasing Sin as apocalyptic power into the world and links that event with human mortality. Paul says nothing about "the fall" or the corruption of human nature because of Adam's sin or about the transmission of Adam's sin through sexual intercourse. Furthermore, Paul's real agenda is not Adam's sin and its consequent universal death, but Messiah Jesus' triumph over the apocalyptic power of

53. See Fredriksen Landes, *Augustine on Romans*, 53.

Sin and gift of righteousness and life for all people. Paul's purpose is to proclaim good news ("the gospel") to Jews and Gentiles in the capital city of the Roman Empire to resolve relational disputes between believers in house churches and to counter imperial propaganda that Caesar Augustus is the "good news" that brings salvation, righteousness, peace, and life to the world. Paul is not concerned to offer an analysis of the origin of evil or sin or how it is propagated in the world.

In short, we should be clear that there is *no* biblical basis for Augustine's doctrine of "original sin." There is no basis for it in the Genesis 3 text, or elsewhere in the Old Testament. There is no basis for it in the New Testament, and certainly not in the locus classicus for Augustine, Romans 5:12. Specifically, there is no biblical evidence for a universal human nature which was forever biologically corrupted by Adam's wilful act and for which all subsequent generations are now accountable. That is, there is no biblical evidence for the notion of "seminal identity" which asserts in one form or another that all humanity was present in Adam's genitals and that an infinitesmal part of Adam's corrupted soul has been transmitted to each subsequent person through the semen of his or her father through the process of sexual intercourse. The Platonic and Stoic foundations for such speculations about the origin and nature of the soul have been abandoned long ago. There is no biblical basis for such a theology, no theological justification for such a theology, and no scientific evidence for such a theology.

The story of the Greek fathers continues to this day in the form of the Greek or Eastern Orthodox Church. This is a church that was profoundly shaped by the theology of Irenaeus, and where Augustine had no influence. The disobedience of Adam and Eve was a result of child-like immaturity rather than wilful intention. There is no such thing as "original sin" or "inherited guilt." Sin is always a personal act, never a function of nature.[54]

One other historical note is important. The Jewish faith, which takes the Hebrew Scriptures as its sacred and normative text, has no theology of original sin.

The bottom line, we should be clear, is that Augustine's doctrine of original sin is without biblical and historical foundation. The doctrine of "original sin," as James O'Donnell states, is Augustine's "most original and

---

54. See, for example, Gonzalez, *Christian Thought Revisited*, 34–49; Meyendorff, *Byzantine Theology*; Ware, *The Orthodox Church*.

nearly single-handed creation."[55] But, as Mark Biddle so succinctly states, "the most fundamental flaw . . ." is that "the doctrine cannot be found in Scripture."[56] It is a mythological creation which the western church has been seduced to believe and teach as dogma.

By the criteria used in the ancient church to differentiate truth from heresy—consistency with the Scripture which by Augustine's time was in canonical form, consistency with the rule of faith (the confessional summaries of the various churches and the major teachers of the churches), consistency with what was taught in all the churches (catholicity)—Augustine's doctrine of original sin was novel to say the least. Augustine's doctrine of original sin could have been declared heretical just as Pelegius' teaching on sin was declared heretical. But Augustine's teaching became dogma instead of heresy, and his teaching has been perpetuated in the western church ever since.

How could a teaching which violated the major criteria for truth in the ancient church become dogma? The truth be told, it had to do with politics, not with what was biblical, or in conformity with the rule of faith, or the catholicity of teaching in all the churches. Augustine, in addition to being a brilliant polemicist, was a strategic politician who knew how to use the power structures of the Roman church as well as the imperial government and its military to serve his theological and ecclesiological purposes, as Pagels and O'Donnell so clearly remind us.[57]

I grew up believing that I was "born in sin" because of Adam's sin in the Garden of Eden. In the spring of 1958 I was taught the doctrine of original sin based on the traducian theory of sin transmission through sexual intercourse by which my father passed on Adam's sin to me. I have now traced the story of the emergence of the doctrine of original sin. It is not taught in the Bible. It is the creation of one man, Augustine, with the help of a few prior teachers in the church, in large part, according to Pelikan and Ferguson, to justify the practice of infant baptism as the means of cleansing for original sin. In other words, the doctrine of original sin is not only without biblical foundation, but it is a late development in the patristic church, and is related to a need undergird an ecclesiastical practice of the western church about which there were some questions in the early church.

55. O'Donnell, *Augustine*, 296.

56. Biddle, *Missing the Mark*, 3.

57. See Pagels, *Adam*, 117–45, especially 117–26, 129, 145; and O'Donnell, *Augustine*, 171–332, especially 225, 263–64, 323–24.

7

Where Do We Go From Here?
Toward a Constructive Proposal

REINHOLD NIEBUHR IS QUOTED often for the line that the one theological doctrine for which there is empirical evidence is the doctrine of sin. The point of this book is not to raise questions about the theology of sin, but to argue that one particular formulation of the theology of sin, namely the doctrine of original sin as articulated by Augustine and then propagated in the history of Christian dogma, is without biblical and theological foundation and merit.

So, what would a theology of sin that rejects Augustine's formulation yet agrees with Niebuhr's observation look like? I submit three proposals as a way to move forward in the church's thinking about sin. First, we need to formulate a biblical theology of sin. That is, we need to try to understand how the people of Israel and then the early followers of Jesus understood sin. Secondly, we need to explore how faith traditions that accept the normativity of the biblical canon (or at least part of it in the case of the Jewish people) but were not shaped by Augustine have interpreted the Genesis 3 story and understood sin. Third, we need to ask how some contemporary theologians have tried to interpret the meaning of sin without embracing the Augustinian formulation.

STARTING WITH THE BIBLE

Sin is a coat of many colors in the Bible. That is, the writers of the Bible use many different words to talk about sin. What are those words and what do they tell us about the understanding of sin among God's people, first in Israel and then among the early followers of Jesus?

The Old Testament Perspective on Sin

Sin was a dominant concern among the theologians of Israel and the writers of the Hebrew Scriptures; over fifty words for "sin" are used in biblical Hebrew if one counts specific as well as generic words.[1] As Elmer Martens points out, the large number of terms for sin indicates the importance of the subject "since in any culture that which is valued or eschewed is differentiated."[2] Old Testament scholars are agreed that of the many words for sin three are critical to defining the Hebrew understanding of sin, *hatta*, *pesa*, *awon*. The first, *hatta*, occurs 595 times in the Hebrew Bible, and at its root means "to miss the mark," "to be mistaken," "to be found deficient." It is first used in Genesis 4:7; God warns Cain that like a wild beast "sin is lurking at the door" and "you must master it." The word is frequently used to express the ethical failure of a person or the "falling short" of expectations in relationships. The theological sense of *hatta* reflects an offense that is committed against God, or a failure that occurs in the sphere of the cult.[3]

The second important word, *pesa*, comes from the political world where it references rebellion and revolt, but also breach. It is used 136 times in the Old Testament, and signifies willful, knowledgeable violation of a norm or standard. It regularly implies the intentional rebellion of an inferior against a superior (e.g., Prov 28:24). It depicts the overstepping of boundaries set by the commandments (e.g., Num 14:41; 1 Sam 15:24). The term is used most frequently in the Old Testament to describe open and brazen human rebellion against or defiance of God. It can also be used to picture a breach or fracturing of relationship, e.g., the brothers of Joseph pleading for his forgiveness by saying "'please forgive the *pesa* ['crime' in

---

1. See Sanders, "Sin, Sinners," *ABD*, Vol. 6, 31. See Knierim, *Die Hauptbegriffe*, for the groundbreaking study on which all subsequent studies are based.

2. Martens, "Sin, Guilt," *Dictionary of the Pentateuch*, 765.

3. See Attridge, "Sin, Sinners," *NIDB*, Vol. 5, 263–75; Kock, "אטח (chata)," *TDOT*, Vol. IV, 309–19; Luc, "אטח (ht)," *NIDOTTE*, Vol 2, 87–93; Martens, "Sin, Guilt," *Dictionary of Pentateuch*, 765–66; for more details and bibliography.

NRSV] of the servants of the God of your father'" (Gen 50:17). "Actions of *pesa* rupture solidarity and shatter harmony," asserts Martens.[4]

The third critical term for sin in the Hebrew Bible, *awon*, occurs 231 times in the Hebrew Scriptures. The word pictures something that is twisted or bent as measured by a standard straight measurement. So, it is defined as "crookedness," "perversity," "iniquity." It has a predominantly religious and ethical connotation, and is almost always used to indicate "crookedness" or "iniquity" before God rather than humans. In the plural form it can serve as the summary term for all human sins against God.[5]

The Old Testament writers describe human sin and evil with a wide range of additional terms—at least 47 other words or images—but the three reviewed, *hatta, pesa, awon*, scholars agree summarize the central theological understandings and concerns about sin in the Hebrew Bible. The richness of the Hebrew lexicon for sin is impressive. The problem of human failure in relationship to God and to fellow human beings is profound and unqualified. What is striking and what all of the concepts for sin have in common is that sin is defined in terms of willful, fractured relationships, broken covenants, rebellion against superiors (God) and fellow-human beings. The term *awon* is often used to summarize what sin is about because it so beautifully yet tragically pictures sin–sin makes crooked, sin distorts reality and relationships, sin creates "disequilibrium," to use a term from Mark Biddle,[6] in an organic model of reality. The whole system is out of balance because of sin, and each individual act of sin only intensifies the intensity of the disequilibrium. Human beings all enter a world that is spinning at near "G" force speed; they lose their balance, they stumble, they miss the mark, they intentionally rebel, and thus each one adds to the intensity of the disequilibrium.

The richness of sin language in the Hebrew Bible indicates that sin is a very complex reality that grows and grows, that gathers speed and throws out of balance unless arrested. The Hebrew faith outlines an elaborate system of atonement to intervene and arrest the spread of sin's growth and the speed of the disequilibrium for individuals and for the collective community, as many studies of the sacrificial system and atonement have

4. Martens, "Sin, Guilt," *Dictionary of the Pentateuch*, 766; see also Attridge, "Sin, Sinners," *NIDB*, Vol. IV, 309–19; Carpenter and Grisanti, "עשׁפ (pesa)," *NIDOTTE*, Vol. 3, 706–10; Sanders, "Sin, Sinners," *ADB*, Vol. 6, 32.

5. See Luc, "ןוָע (awon)," *NIDOTTE*, Vol. 3, 351; Martens, "Sin, Guilt," *Dictionary of the Pentateuch*, 767; Sanders, "Sin, Sinners," *ABD*, Vol. 6, 32.

6. Biddle, *Missing the Mark*, xii. Biddle's book is a very healthy corrective to the Augustinian and classic Western understanding of sin.

documented. But even then, atonement and forgiveness cannot interrupt the life cycle of all sin (s).

The bottom line is that the theologians of Israel believed that sin was the willful mistrust of God, rebellion against God, breach of relationship with fellow human beings. Sin was understood in relational terms. They had not heard of Augustine nor of the doctrine of "original sin." There is not a hint in the Hebrew Bible of sin as an ontological reality that is transmitted biologically from one generation to the next via sexual intercourse, as proposed by Augustine.

The New Testament Perspective on Sin

The writers of the New Testament do not write about sin as much as the writers of the Hebrew Scriptures; they use fewer words and use them less often. There are seven words—"unrighteous" (*adikia*) [twenty-five times], "sin" (*hamartia*) [173 times: sixty-four in Paul, forty-eight of which are in Romans], "lawless" (*anomia*) [fourteen times], "ungodly" (*asebia*) [six times], "transgression" (*parabasis*) [seven times], "disobey" (*parakoe*) [three times], "fall beside" (*paraptoma*) [nineteen times]—which are translated as "sin" 247 times in total. The noun *adikia*, translated as "unrighteous" or "unjust," occurs twenty-five times in the New Testament and denotes unjust actions in relations to other human beings. Paul uses it in Romans 1:29 as a comprehensive term at the head of the vice list which follows; it defines what unjust behavior in the vice list looks like. It is the exact opposite of righteousness (*dikaiosune*). The criterion for defining unrighteous or unjust action is the righteousness of God (Rom 3:5, 26). The most commonly used word for sin in the New Testament is *hamartia*. It basically meant to "miss the mark," and in first century Judaism (both BCE and CE) it denoted primarily two things: 1) a falling away from a relationship of faithfulness to God, and 2) a falling away from obedience to the commandments of the law. This is the common understanding of the word "sin" that is reflected in the writings of the New Testament. The word used in the plural, sins, (*hamartiai*), refers to acts of sin. In the Synoptic Gospels the word is found almost exclusively in the context of the forgiveness of sins, that is, behaviors or attitudes which are sinful.[7] The word is transformed into an apocalyptic power in the writings of Paul; it is used in the singular and personified.[8] "Lawless" (*anomia*) pictures social chaos

---

7. See W. Guenther, "Sin," *NIDNTT*, Vol. 3, 577–80.

8. See the discussion of Paul's apocalyptic theology of sin in chapter 3.

because people break the law, the law of God and civic laws. Another form of sin is irreverence toward God or "ungodliness" (*asebia*). Paul links such irreverence toward God and injustice in Romans 1:18. Jude and 2 Peter describe followers of Jesus as the righteous who live like Noah and Lot in the midst of ungodly people (*asebeis*) (Jude 4, 15, 18; 2 Pet 2:5f.; 3:7). "Transgression" means to "walk across the line" or "go beside the line." It pictures a deviation from an original and true direction. The word is used primarily in the letters of Paul to refer to Jewish transgression of the law to make the point that Jewish people are sinners before God just as are Gentile peoples (e.g., Rom 2:17–29). One of the most interesting words for sin in the New Testament is the word "disobedience" (*parakoe*). It literally means "to hear beside" or "not to hear." The person who does not hear does not obey. In Romans 5:19 it refers to Adam's disobedience of God, in 2 Corinthians 10:6 to the Corinthians disobedience of Paul, and in Hebrews 2:2 to human disobedience of the word of God spoken through angels. "Fall beside," *paraptoma*, has a very similar meaning. It denotes falling beside the right way and thus transgressing or erring. Used exclusively in Matthew and Paul, the word emphasizes a deliberate act through which a person loses the relationship with God that he/she has. In Romans 5:18 Adam's sinful action led to the condemnation of all human beings.

The language of sin in the New Testament describes human beings making choices, wrong choices, unjust choices that harm other people, choices that lead them astray, choices that result in personal and communal chaos, choices that reflect irreverence toward God, choices that mean disobedience toward God, choices that miss the mark of God's intention for them. But they are choices that human beings make. Paul says it so clearly, "all [people] have sinned and fallen short of the glory of God" (Rom 3:23). A little earlier in the same letter he explains why all have sinned and fallen short, "all people, Jews and Gentiles, are under the power of sin" (Rom 3:9). Sin is universal because all people are enslaved to powers which disorient, which destabilize, which fracture individuals, the social order and the cosmos itself. There is relational estrangement, people make wrong choices because they are enslaved to an apocalyptic power. The deeper problem in the world is a political one, it is a question of kingship or rulership. Human beings are subject to "principalities and powers" from which they need liberation or redemption from a liberator or redeemer who was faithful where Adam mistrusted and who was obedient where Adam was disobedient. Sin language in the New Testament is volitional, relational, and political. There is no hint of ontological corruption; in fact, the language of ontology is completely absent.

To underline the volitional and political nature of sin language in the New Testament, various early Christian theologians emphasize that one man, Messiah Jesus, "had to be made like his brethren in every respect" (Heb 2:17) and "in every respect has been tempted as we are, yet without sin [*hamartia*]" (Heb 5:15). Or, in the Pauline contrast, "as one man's trespass led to condemnation of all men, so by one man's righteous act righteousness of life was granted to all men," and as one man's disobedience" made many sinners, so "one man's obedience" will make many righteous (Rom 5:18–19). Adam chose to sin. Jesus chose not to sin. Jesus was a good Jew who believed that the law was doable, as Deuteronomy 30:11–14 taught, and he walked the talk. We do not need the neo-Platonic metaphysics of Nicea or Chalcedon or the neo-Platonic ontology of Augustine to explain why Jesus could be "like his brethren in every respect" and be "tempted as we are, yet without sin."

The writers of the Old and New Testament use many different words to talk about the reality of sin which readers of the English Bible tend to miss because this diversity gets translated with one word, "sin." Sin is falling short of expectations in relationship with God and fellow humans, it is rebelling against God and breaking relationships with other humans, it is overstepping the boundaries set by God or the community, it is breaking agreements with God and others, it is crookedness in relationships or agreements with God and others, it is injustice in relationships, it is disobedience in relationship to God and the community, it is ungodliness in relationship to God. Sin is all of these things because people make wrong choices because they have permitted their lives to come under the influence and control of social, institutional, and transpersonal or transcendent powers.

Mark Biddle was correct, the doctrine of original sin as formulated by Augustine and taught as dogma in the western church since the Council of Orange (529) "cannot be found in Scripture."[9]

SOME ECCLESIAL OPTIONS

There are some faith traditions that affirm the normativity of the biblical canon, and thus the Genesis 3 story, but they have not been shaped by the Augustinian understanding of sin. The theologies of sin in these traditions

9. Biddle, *Missing the Mark*, 3.

point the way forward toward a constructive understanding of sin. Three such traditions are identified in what follows.

The Jewish Tradition

The Jewish faith shares the Hebrew Bible or the Old Testament with the Christian church. The Jewish community thus reads and interprets the story of Adam and Eve's disobedience in Genesis 3 together with all Christians. But there is no doctrine of original sin in Judaism's understanding of the Genesis 3 story. How does the Jewish tradition interpret the Genesis 3 narrative? The Jewish interpretation of Genesis 3 centers around two themes. First, the disobedience of Adam and Eve brought death and mortality. It established the fundamental principle that sin results in punishment.[10] Second, the expulsion from the Garden became a metaphor in Judaism for exile and for exilic existence. *Galut*, exile, became the paradigmatic metaphor for the story of the Jewish people. Adam and Eve leaving the Garden prefigured Israel's exile in Babylon. But between the bookends of Eden and Babylon there are many other experiences that the Jewish people interpret through the paradigm of exile, e.g., Abraham and Sarah in Egypt, Jacob in servitude to Laban, and Jacob and his descendants oppressed in Egypt until liberated by Moses. The loss of homeland and Temple as a result of the Jewish-Roman War of 66–70 was interpreted as another historic and theological exile. Through the long, difficult and painful history of antiquity, the Middle Ages, and modernity the Jewish people hope and pray for an end to exile and a return to a homeland. In modern times exile has become an existential metaphor for the rights of personhood and the promise of a metaphoric homecoming to meaning and wholeness.[11]

So, what happens to sin in Jewish thinking? The Jewish theology of sin is anchored in Genesis 4:7, "sin crouches at the door," and Genesis 8:21, "the devisings [*yetzer*] of man's heart are evil from his youth." Human beings struggle with two tendencies, a good *yetzer* and an evil *yetzer*, and they must make choices with the help of the Torah and the grace of God to choose to follow the good *yetzer* and repent when they fail to do so.[12]

10. See Kepnes, "Sin and Repentance," 295.

11. See Hoffman, "Principle, Story and Myth," 242–44; and Kepnes, "Sin and Repentance," 295–96.

12. See Kepnes, "Sin and Repentance, 295, and Zoloth, "Exile and Return, especially 307. In her response to Kepnes, Zoloth focuses on sin as "error" (*chet*) in Jewish

The Eastern Orthodoxy Tradition

The Eastern Orthodox interpretation of the Christian faith grew out of the Greek or eastern wing of the early church. Its paradigmatic theologian was Irenaeus.[13] Its theology of sin was untouched by Augustine. The Eastern Orthodox Church thus has not and does not teach the doctrine of original sin as formulated by Augustine and taught in the western church.

Following the lead of Irenaeus, the Eastern Orthodox tradition does not read the story of Genesis 3 and the history of human sinfulness in the context of "a fall" from a state of "Original Righteousness" and "Perfection." In fact, Adam and Eve were created imperfect in order to become perfect through stages of growth and maturity. Adam and Eve's disobedience in the Garden interrupted the process of maturation that God had ordained for them. Humanity's "fallen" state represents a kind of arrested development. Even before "the fall" and in spite of not having sinned, Adam and Eve needed salvation because they were imperfect and incomplete children. The goal of the process of maturation always was and remains Christ.[14]

The sin of Adam and Eve was caused by a premature attempt to gain the knowledge of good and evil instead of as originally intended by a gradual process through educational stages. Adam's choice was a personal choice and act, not a collective one. The punishment was death. There was no collective guilt nor a "sin of nature." Hence, according to a virtual consensus among the Greek fathers, "inherited guilt is impossible."[15] Therefore, sin in the Eastern Orthodox Church is always a personal act. According to John Meyendorff, one of the leading twentieth century Eastern Orthodox theologians in North America, "the belief in a 'sin of nature' is a heresy."[16]

The biblical basis for this interpretation of sin is a very different translation and interpretation of the Romans 5:12 text that was so foundational for Augustine and the western tradition. While, as we have seen,

theology. Sin concerns acts, especially acts of injustice toward the vulnerable; sin does not lie in the nature of the individual.

13. See chapter 4.

14. See Tsirpanlis, *Eastern Patristic Thought*, 47–49, based on Irenaeus, *Against Heresies*, 2.25.3; 4.11.1; see also Biddle, *Missing the Mark*, 5.

15. Tsirpanlis, *Eastern Patristic Thought*, 52. See also Meyendorff, *Byzantine Theology*, 143; and Ware, *Orthodox Church*, 222–23.

16. Meyendorff, *Byzantine Theology*, 143, who cites the Patristic Patriarch Photius in support of his assertion.

The Story of Original Sin

Augustine following Ambrosiaster translated the *eph ho pantes hemarton* phrase in Romans 5:12 as "in whom [i.e., Adam] all men have sinned" to justify the doctrine of inherited guilt from Adam and its spread to all his descendants, the Greek fathers translated the phrase as "because all men have sinned" and interpreted it to mean that in fact all human beings sinned just as Adam had sinned. And all men paid the penalty for their sin, death, just as Adam did. Lest anyone think that this interpretation of Romans 5:12 diminishes the significance of Adam's sin, Meyendorff adds this important interpretive comment, "it presupposes a cosmic significance of the sin of Adam, but does not say that his descendants are 'guilty,' as he was, unless they also sin as he sinned."[17]

In addition to introducing death as a punishment for personal sin, Adam's sin did "cut off" humanity from God and place his descendants under the dominion of sin and the devil. Each human being is now born into a world where sin prevails everywhere, and where it is easy to do evil and difficult to do the good. The human will has been weakened, the human mind has been darkened so that humans can no longer hope to attain to the likeness of God. But the Eastern Orthodox do not go as far as Augustine and the Western tradition and say that Adam's sin deprived humanity entirely of God's grace, or that they are completely depraved of good desires. They disagreed with Augustine's claim that humans are under "'a harsh necessity' to commit sin, and that 'human nature was overcome by the fault into which it fell, *and so came to lack freedom*.'"[18] In other words, the image of God in humans is distorted by sin, but not destroyed. Eastern Orthodox to this day still sing at funeral services that "I am the image of Your inexpressible glory, even though I bear the wounds of sin."[19] Because humans still retain the image of God, they remain free, although the range of that freedom is restricted by sin.

The contrast with the western tradition is focused sharply on the question of baptism. Augustine argued for infant baptism by a very literal interpretation of the Nicean Creed, "baptism for the remission of sin." On the basis of his interpretation of Romans 5:12, children were born sinful, not because they had sinned personally, but because they had sinned "in Adam." Their baptism was necessary for "the remission" of inherited sins. Eastern Orthodox theologians contemporary with Augustine denied

---

17. Ibid., 144.

18. Ware, *Orthodox Church*, 223. The citation of Augustine is from *On the Perfection of Man's Righteousness*, iv.9.

19. Ware, *Orthodox Church*, 224.

that the creedal formula applied to infant baptism. The church baptized children to give them a new and immortal life, not to "remit their yet non-existent sins." Infants need the baptism of immortal life because their mortal parents could not give that to them. The opposition between the two Adams was seen in terms not of guilt and forgiveness, as in the western church, but of death and life. The critical text for the eastern church was 1 Corinthians 15:47–48: "The first man was from the earth, a man of dust; the second man is from heaven. As was the man of dust so are those who are of the dust; and as is the man of heaven, so are those who are of heaven." Baptism is "a liberation, because it gives access to the new immortal life brought into the world by Christ's Resurrection."[20]

The divide between the Greek Orthodox tradition and the western Catholic and Protestant understandings of the Genesis 3 story, Romans 5:12, and original sin are wide. But the Eastern Orthodox tradition does offer a healthy corrective to the western tradition that deserves more considered thought in the West. It has no notion of the first humans as originally righteous and perfect, which is without biblical foundation. The eastern translation and its interpretation of Romans 5:12 is one which almost all modern New Testament scholars affirm. It's theology of the incarnation of Christ is not framed as God's response to human sin, but rather as part of God's plan from eternity to bring salvation to humanity and the cosmos. It affirms Christlikeness through *theosis* or deification as humanity's true and original goal.[21]

The Eastern Orthodox Church has witnesses significant growth, especially a migration of young people from conservative and evangelical churches, since the late twentieth century. It's more constructive anthropology as well as its emphasis on tradition seem attractive to younger people seeking a sense of meaning in a postmodern world.

The Anabaptism-Mennonite Tradition

The Anabaptist-Mennonite reform movement in the sixteenth century broke with the Augustinian Catholic and Protestant interpretation of original sin. In fact, the Anabaptists avoided the term "original sin" because it is not found in the Scriptures. Secondly, the Anabaptists rejected the notion of "original sin" because Ezekiel 18:4 explicitly states that "it

20. Meyendorff, *Byzantine Theology*, 146.

21. See Gonzalez, *Christian Thought*, 34–49; Clendenin, *Eastern Orthodox Christianity*, 120–23; Biddle, *Missing the Mark*, 5–7, for similar and additional comparisons.

is only the person who sins that shall die" and verse 20 teaches that "the person who sins shall die. A child shall not suffer for the iniquity of a parent, nor a parent suffer for the iniquity of a child; the righteousness of the righteous shall be his own, and the wickedness of the wicked shall be his own."[22] The Ezekiel reference was particularly significant for the Anabaptists, says Robert Friedman, because it freed the movement from the "fatalistic character" of "inherited sin" which was so characteristic of the Catholic Church and Protestant orthodoxy.

While rejecting the concept of original sin, the Anabaptists believed that the sin of Adam and Eve was real and introduced into the world a powerful tendency or inclination to sin which resulted in universal sinfulness, but it was a sinfulness by choice rather than by nature. The sin of Adam and Eve did not change the essence or nature of humanity. The consequence of the sin in Eden was moral, not ontological, that is, inherent in human nature.[23] After Genesis 3 each individual has his or her individual "fall," just as did Adam and Eve.[24] Because the sin of Adam and Eve did not alter human nature, the Anabaptists believed that human beings retained the image of God and have free will to choose to sin or to obey God. The repeated call to repentance and to be "born again" is testimony to their deep conviction in freedom of the will and what Richard Weingart calls peoples ability to "cooperate with God's grace in freely entering the kingdom of Christ in obedient discipleship."[25]

With the rejection of original sin the Anabaptists also rejected the practice of infant baptism. On this issue all the Anabaptists groups were unanimous. According to Pilgrim Marpeck, one of the leading theologians of the sixteenth century movement, the ascription of "original sin to infants is the invention of the sophist himself, and is without any basis in Scripture," and, therefore, the idea that baptism will cleanse the child is completely without merit.[26] Children, the Anabaptists believed, were born "with the purity of creation, unaware of good and evil . . ."[27] Until the "age of discernment of good and evil" children were considered innocent and saved by the redeeming work of Christ. Whatever wrongs the children

22. See Williams, *Spiritual and Anabaptist Writers*, 127; and Friedman, "Doctrine of Original Sin," 208. See also Kaufman, "Sin," 824.

23. See Dyck, "Sinners and Saints," 89–93.

24. See Keeney, *Dutch Anabaptist Thought*, 68–69.

25. Weingart, "Meaning of Sin," 31; see also Friedman, "Doctrine of Original Sin," 213.

26. *Writings of Marpeck*, 210.

27. Ibid., 246.

had committed prior to the "age of discernment" were not "imputed" to them "for Jesus sake."[28] Children, therefore, could not be called sinners. The Anabaptists paid a high price for this stance; it was considered heretical by both Catholics and Protestants, and many were martyred for their rejection of infant baptism and commitment to adult baptism only on the voluntary confession of faith.

The rejection of the idea of original sin and the practice of infant baptism by the sixteenth century Anabaptists has been continued to this day by their heirs now known primarily as Mennonites. A study of the confessional tradition of the three largest Mennonite bodies documents the absence of "original sin" language–the Dordrecht Confession of 1632 and the Mennonite Confession of Faith of 1963 of the Mennonite General Conference; the Ris Confession of 1766 and 1895, and the Common Confession of 1933 of the General Conference of Mennonite Churches; the Mennonite Brethren Confession of Faith of 1902, and the Confession of Faith of the Mennonite Brethren Churches of 1976.[29] The most recent confessional statements, following years of leadership and congregational study, reflect the on-going commitment to understand the theology of sin in non-Augustinian terms. *The Confession of Faith in a Mennonite Perspective*, the confession of the merged Mennonite Church and the General Conference Mennonite Church which constitutes the largest Mennonite Church in North America, makes the following confessional statement:

> We confess that, beginning with Adam and Eve, humanity has disobeyed God, given way to the tempter, and chosen to sin. Because of sin, all have fallen short of the Creator's intent, marred the image of God in which they were created, disrupted order in the world, and limited their love for others. Because of sin, humanity has been given over to the enslaving powers of evil and death.[30]

The confession of the Mennonite Brethren Church, the second largest Mennonite Church in North America reads as follows:

> We believe that the first humans yielded to the tempter and fell into sin. Since then, all people disobey God and choose to sin, falling short of the glory of God. As a result, sin and evil have gained a hold in the world, disrupting God's purposes for the

28. See Weingart, "Meaning of Sin," 30–31; Friedman, "Doctrine of Original Sin," 209.

29. See Loewen, One Lord..., for accessible copies of these confessional documents.

30. Confession of Faith in Mennonite Perspective, 31.

created order and alienating humans from God and thus from creation, each other and themselves. Human sinfulness results in physical and spiritual death. Because all have sinned, all face eternal separation from God.[31]

Since 1525 one Protestant body of Christians have believed and evangelized on the basis of a different anthropology than that articulated by Augustine and the majority of western Christians and churches. As the larger culture in the West has moved into a post-Christendom and a post-denominational socio-religious reality, more and more Christians and "seekers" are finding the larger "ecclesial stream" represented by the Anabaptist tradition with its peacemaking teachings and practices an attractive alternative.

SOME CONTEMPORARY THEOLOGICAL OPTIONS

Many contemporary theologians continue to talk and write about sin, some in traditional Augustinian terms while others seek to formulate constructive alternative ways of understanding sin. Some of these theologians are sampled for contemporary modes of thinking about sin.

Re-Affirm Augustine

One wing of the evangelical church in North America continues to re-affirm Augustine's doctrine of original sin. For example. Donald Bloesch, the "Dean of evangelical theologians" in the last quarter of the twentieth century whose *Essentials of Evangelical Theology* was widely used in evangelical seminaries, claims that it was Augustine "who rediscovered the biblical doctrine of total depravity and gave it the recognition it deserves. He spoke of 'the entire mass of our nature' being 'ruined beyond doubt' and falling 'into the possession of its destroyer.'"[32] Or, in today's widely used *Systematic Theology: An Introduction to Biblical Doctrine*, Wayne Grudem contends that all humans inherit sin and legal guilt directly from Adam. In addition, he contents that all humans "inherit a sinful nature because of Adam's sin."[33] Bloesch and Grudem are certain that Augustine interpreted Romans 5:12 correctly despite the fact that there is strong

31. Confession of Faith . . . Mennonite Brethren Churches, 10.
32. Bloesch, *Essentials*, Vol. 1, 90–91.
33. Grudem, *Systematic Theology*, 496.

agreement among New Testament scholars that Augustine's reading of the text, which, we have noted, he based on Ambrosiaster's mistranslation and misinterpretation of that text, is incorrect. So, the first problem that this group of evangelical theologians have to address is that their systematic theology is seriously out of sync with the Biblical teaching which they claim to faithfully interpret. Secondly, these theologians are making a series of assumptions about human nature, including the relationship of body and soul, and the transmission of sin which are challengeable on both biblical and scientific grounds.[34] As O'Donnell stated so well, "what ever becomes of 'soul' will determine what becomes of Augustine."[35] He goes on to note that contemporary cognitive sciences are challenging the deepest western assumptions about human nature. Third, we must ask how these theologians are going to address the mounting scientific and anthropological evidence for polygenism—the emergence of the human race from multiple parents in multiple parts of the world.[36] This evidence raises profound questions about the reading of the Genesis creation narrative as an historical account which records the monogenesis of the human race–the human race emerged from a single set of parents. Polygenism represents a significant challenge for an Augustinian view of original sin.

A Wink and a Nod

There is another group of contemporary theologians who recognize that Augustine's theology of sin is problematic, but they tip the hat to him while offering a rich phenomenological description of sin that is not dependent on him.

Alistair McFadyen, Senior Lecturer in Theology at the University of Leeds in the United Kingdom, has been selected to illustrate the point. McFadyen analyses the problem of sin language in the context of a European culture where sin language "has fallen into disuse in general public (but also in much Christian and theological) discourse as a language for talking about the pathological in human affairs."[37] McFadyen wants to rehabilitate sin language because he thinks it is critical to understand

---

34. See, for example, Green, *Body, Soul, and Human Life*, and the bibliography he references.

35. O'Donnell, *Augustine*, 326.

36. See, for example, Graves, *The Emperor's New Clothes*; Livingston, *Adam's Ancestors*; Kasujja, *Polygenism and Original Sin*.

37. *Bound to Sin*, 3.

sin theologically in a secular and pragmatically atheistic culture. If sin at its core is a disorientation and disruption of humans proper relationship with God, it is critically important that the pathologies identified in the modern world be defined in relationship to God.[38] McFadyen recognizes the enormity of the challenge. The resistance of modernity to the doctrine of original sin is strong, sustained, and widespread for multiple reasons: 1) its reliance on the historicity of the account Adam and Eve's sin in Genesis 3; 2) its biological determinism–all humans inherited Adam's sin before they were born and before they could act sinfully; 3) its assumption of monogenism, the descent of all humans from a single pair of ancestors; 4) its fundamental challenge to the ontology of modernity, that the individual is autonomous and that autonomy is the sole basis for establishing responsibility and guilt.[39]

After providing two detailed case studies of more extreme cases of sin, one on the sexual abuse of children and the second on "The Final Solution and the binding of reason" (the German holocaust against the Jewish people), McFadyen tries to make the case for the doctrine of original sin through the concept of "the bondage of the will" with full acknowledgment of his indebtedness to Martin Luther and Jonathan Edwards.[40] With the help of feminist theologians and Augustine, McFadyen argues that the human will or intentionality is not free and autonomous as modern ontology wants to believe. It is disoriented and confused either by powerful ideologies and relational or situational dynamics in feminism or by original sin in Augustine. The human will is bound; it "constricts and restricts human beings from being-in-relation which is proper to them" which is precisely the definition of sin and it is that before any actions. Augustine in the end, according to McFayden, was correct when he spoke of an inherited corruption of the dynamics of willing. All sins are acts of will which is the result of an inherited disorientation that is always already within; it has been communicated biologically and received at conception. No one enters the world in a state of innocence; "the dynamics of our willing are from the outset already disoriented."[41]

McFadyen makes a valiant effort to rehabilitate Augustine and his doctrine of original sin, but there is a huge disconnect between his analysis

38. See Ibid., 3–12.

39. Ibid., 14–33.

40. See Ibid., 110, for reference to Luther's *Bondage of the Will* written against Erasmus and Edwards *Freedom of the Will* written to oppose New England Arminianism.

41. McFayden, *Bound to Sin*, 190.

of sin, especially the perceptive discussion of the case studies as well as the feminist theological critiques of traditional Christian understandings of sin, and his appeal to Augustine. Even McFadyen admits near the end of the book that while his "claim of biological transmission has not been amenable to testing in relation to these pathologies [e.g., child abuse and holocaust], it is clear that this disorientation is transmittable through the dynamics of social relationships."[42] McFadyen makes the latter case much stronger than the former. It is significantly harder to talk persuasively and theologically about sin in Augustinian terms in the post-Christendom West of the twenty-first century than it is to talk persuasively and theologically about sin as disorientation that is transmitted through the dynamics of structural and social relationships.

Moving Past Augustine

A series of Christian theologians in North America have chosen to address the question of sin theologically without reference to Augustine's concept of original sin. Several theologians are cited as pointers of the way forward for the Christian community.

Cornelius Plantinga, a professor of theology at Calvin Theological Seminary and a minister at the Woodlawn Christian Reformed Church in Grand Rapids, Michigan, offers a wonderful discussion of sin under the title *Not the Way It's Supposed to Be. A Breviary of Sin*. The book won the *Christianity Today* 1996 Book of the Year award. Plantinga outlines a criteriological approach to sin rather than an ontological one; that is, he defines "what is sinful" rather than "what is sin."[43] What God desires is shalom, universal flourishing, wholeness, delight. Shalom, often translated as peace, "is the way things ought to be."[44] Sin is shalom-breaking; it is whatever disturbs the shalom that God has designed. Plantinga then offers a rich and troubling menu of the things that humans and societies do to disturb, pervert, corrupt, disintegrate, and shatter shalom.

James McClendon, the late scholar-in-residence at Fuller Theological Seminary, asserts without equivocation that "'original sin' . . . is not the teaching of Scripture. It rests upon historic but mistaken readings."[45] He proceeds to outline an alternative understanding of sin, what he calls "the

42. Ibid., 246–47.
43. Plantinga, *Not the Way*, 13.
44. Ibid., 10.
45. McClendon, *Theology*, Vol. 2, 125.

baptist vision" (small "b"), under three rubrics. First, sin is refusal—the opposition to the new creation, the *anastatic* vision of all things new, the new world (*kaine ktisis*, 2 Cor 5:17) that Jesus brings into the world. One corollary of this principle, according to McClendon, is that there is no reason to impute mortal sins to people who have not received the good news of the gospel. Sin is refusal of the proffered good news, which such people have not committed.[46] Second, sin is rupture—the break of relationships among humans made for company with one another and for fellowship with God. Sin is social; it disrupts what God is setting right in Jesus Christ.[47] Third, sin is reversion—it rejects "the good proper to organic life and growth" in the "ecological story of life in our biosphere."[48]

Stanley Grenz, the late professor of theology at Carey Theological College and Regent College in Vancouver, British Columbia, seeks to understand sin in communal terms. Since human creation in the image of God means reflecting the nature of God, who is a social Trinity, sin is ultimately the disruption of community with God, fellow human beings and the created order. Sin as failure, that is, missing the mark or "falling short of the glory of God" finds its ultimate expression in the fracturing and destruction of community. Grenz wants to retain the term "original sin" with the understanding that it refers to the "first sin" which introduced sin into the world, not to the biological transmission of sin in the Augustinian sense of the term. That first sin destroyed the primordial experience of community which immediately marred the divine image and functioned like the proverbial rock in the pond in human history; it sent out wave after wave of disruptive consequences for all the descendants of Adam and Eve that are so corrosive that he wants to talk about inheriting a depraved nature by heredity and socialization, but one that does not directly entail personal guilt. The results of sin for human beings are: 1) alienation in all relationships, and thus the loss of community; 2) condemnation before the righteousness of God; 3) enslavement to a cosmic power that binds the will; 4) depravity that deprives humans of the ability to remedy their own situation.[49]

Thomas Finger, a Mennonite theologian, defines sin as "a massive corporate power, or interweaving of interrelated powers which opposes God on all social, religious, and personal levels, seeking to bring all

46. Ibid., 130–31.
47. Ibid., 132–33.
48. Ibid., 133–34.
49. Grenz, *Theology for Community*, 268–75.

creation under the dominion of death."[50] For humans sin expresses itself in turning the heart from God in specific acts and relationships by turning towards forces opposed to God and getting involved in acts and relationships which these forces promote. Sin then involves a "collusion with and bondage under corporate powers of evil who oppose God's call."[51] Humans bear responsibility for their sin because they cooperate with these powers. Sin is transmitted from generation to generation not through biological means as in Augustine but by the powers through the social, institutional, and transpersonal dynamics.

CONCLUSION

The language we use is important. I agree with McFayden that it is imperative that the Christian church use the language of sin rather than the language of pathology to talk theologically, psychologically, and sociologically about the human condition. The real human problem is deeper than illness which can be healed through therapy or medical intervention.[52] It is a profound enslavement, estrangement, alienation, disequilibrium from and with God, the core of one's center, fellow human beings, nature, the cosmos from which humans and the cosmos need redemption from the eternal God who created and loves humanity and the creation. No language in the human lexicon describes the human condition and crisis more accurately than sin. No other word more clearly communicates the personal, interpersonal, communal, ethical, political, ecological, cosmological and theological quality of the human and creational brokeness of reality. The Christian church cannot surrender the language of sin without defanging the gospel of its power.

Precisely because language matters, I disagree with Grenz proposal to continuing using "original sin" language to refer to the first sin of Adam and Eve in the Garden but not to the Augustinian definition of sin as biologically transmitted from generation to generation. The Augustinian understanding of sin has so damaged the language of "original sin" that its

---

50. Finger, *Theology*, Vol. 2, 159.

51. Ibid., 160. Finger is clear that when he refers to the powers or forces he is thinking of the Pauline concept of the "principalities and powers," that is both the powers of sociological structures and transpersonal or transcendent powers.

52. I recognize that some psychological pathologies are passed on genetically, and require medical intervention. For the importance of being multi-lingual, see Taylor, *Speaking of sin*; and Dueck, "Speaking the Languages of Sin," 20–21.

usefulness is now spent. We must use sin language but abandon "original sin" language.

So, how do we understand sin? Sin is enslavement to transpersonal and structural powers, the "power of sin" or the "principalities and powers" to use Pauline language, that have the world and humans in their grip. All humans are born into the world that is enslaved by these powers, that is in the disequilibrium created by these powers, and we all let ourselves be seduced by these powers or we choose to embrace these powers and their sinful ways. Each culture and each ideology gives expression to these powers in different ways, so that the Christian church must continually discern the ways in which the powers tempt and call people to chose to turn away from God, each other, and creation.

We close with Paul, one of the earliest theologians of the Jesus movement: "all people . . . are under the power of sin" (Rom 3:9), and "all people have sinned and fallen short of the glory of God" (Rom 3:23). The language is volitional and political, not ontological.

Bibliography

PRIMARY SOURCES

Ambrose. *Apologia prophetae David* [A Defense of the Prophet David]. Vol. 14, *Patrologia Latina*, edited by J. P. Migne. Paris: Migne, 1844–64.

———. "Death as a Good." *Seven Exegetical Works*. Vol. 65, *The Fathers of the Church*. Washington, DC: Catholic University of America Press, 1971.

———. *Expositio evaangelii secundum Lucan* [A Commentary on the Gospel according to Luke]. Vol. 15, *Patrologia Latina*, edited by J. P. Migne. Paris: Migne, 1844–64.

———. *Expositio in Psalmum cxviii* [A Commentary on Psalm 118]. Vol. 15, *Patrologia Latina*, edited by J. P. Migne. Paris: Migne, 1844–64.

———. *The Mysteries*. Vol. 44, *The Fathers of the Church*. Washington, DC: Catholic University of America Press, 1963.

———. *On the Belief in the Resurrection*. Vol. 10, *Nicene and Post-Nicene Fathers, Ambrose: Selected Works and Letters*. Reprint. Peabody, MA: Henrickson, 2004.

———. *On the Death of Satyrus*. Vol. 10, *Nicene and Post-Nicene Fathers, Ambrose: Selected Works and Letters*. Reprint. Peabody, MA: Henrickson, 2004.

Ambrosiaster. *Commentaries on Romans and 1–2 Corinthians*. Ancient Christian Texts. Translated by Gerald L. Bray. Downers Grove, IL: InterVarsity Press, 2009.

———. *Commentari Romanos. Ambrosiastri Qui dicitur Commentarius in Epistulas Paulinas*. 3 vols. Edited by H. J. Vogels. Corpus Scriptorum Ecclesasitcorum Latinorum. Vienna: Hoelder-Pichler-Tempsky, 1966.

Augustine. *A Treatise on the Grace of Christ, and on Original Sin*. Vol. 5, *Nicene and Post-Nicene Fathers*. Reprint. Peabody, MA: Hendrickson, 2004.

———. *Against Julian*. Vol. 35, *The Fathers of the Church*. Washington, DC: Catholic University of America Press, 1957.

———. *Answer to Julian, Answer to the Pelagians*. Vol. 2, *The Works of St. Augustine*. Hyde Park, NY: New City, 1998.

———. *City of God*. 2 Vols. Loeb Classical Library. Cambridge: Harvard University Press, 1966.

———. *Confessions*. 2 Vols., Loeb Classical Library. Cambridge: Harvard University Press, 1968.

———. *Eighty-Three Different Questions*. Vol. 70, *The Fathers of the Church*. Washington, DC: Catholic University Press of America, 1977.

———. *Faith, Hope, and Charity* (also known as *Enchiridion*). Vol. 3, *Ancient Christian Writers*. New York: Newman, n.d.

———. *Marriage and Desire, Answer to the Pelagians*. Vol. 2, *The Works of St. Augustine*. Hyde Park, NY: New City, 1998.

———. *On the Grace of Christ, and On Original Sin*. Vol. 5, *Nicene and Post-Nicene Fathers*. Reprint. Peabody, MA: Hendrickson, 2004.

———. *On the Soul and Its Origin*. Vol. 5, *Nicene and Post-Nicene Fathers*. Reprint. Peabody, MA: Hendrickson, 2004.

———. *The Forgiveness of Sins and the Baptism of the Little Ones, Answer to the Pelagians*. Vol. 1, *The Works of St. Augustine*. Hyde Park, NY: New City, 1997.

———. *Letters*. Vol. 3 (131–164). *The Fathers of the Church*. Washington, DC: Catholic University of America Press, 1953.

———. *Letters*. Vol. 4 (165–203). *The Fathers of the Church*. Washington, DC: Catholic University of America Press, 1955.

———. *The Literal Meaning of Genesis*. 2 Vols. *Ancient Christian Writers*, New York: Newman, 1982.

———. *To Simplician—On Various Questions*. Book I, *Augustine: Early Writings*. Vol. VI, *Library of Christian Classics*. Philadelphia: Westminster, 1953.

Chrysostom, John. *The Homilies of St. John Chrysostom on the Epistle of St. Paul the Apostle to the Romans*. Vol. 11, *Nicene and Post-Nicene Fathers*. Reprint. Peabody, MA: Hendrickson, 2004.

Clement of Alexandria. *Protreptikos*. Vol. 2, *Ante-Nicene Fathers*. Reprint. Peabody, MA: Hendrickson, 1999.

———. *The Stromata*. Vol. 2, *Ante-Nicene Fathers*. Reprint. Peabody, MA: Hendrickson, 1999.

Cyprian. "Letter 64." *Letters 1–81*. Vol. 51, *The Fathers of the Church*. Washington, DC: Catholic University of America Press, 1964.

Irenaeus. *Against Heresies*. Vol. 1, *Ante-Nicene Fathers*. Reprint. Peabody, MA: Hendrickson, 1999.

———. *Proof of the Apostolic Preaching*. Vol. 16, *Ancient Christian Writers*. New York: Newman, 1952.

Fourth Book of Ezra. Translated by B. M. Metzger. Vol. 1, *The Old Testament Pseudepigrapha*. Edited by James H. Charlesworth. Garden City, NY: Doubleday, 1985.

Jubilees. Translated by O. S. Wintermute. Vol. 2, *The Old Testament Pseudepigrapha*. Edited by James H. Charlesworth. Garden City, NY: Doubleday, 1985,

Justin Martyr. *Dialogue with Trypho*. *The Writings of Justin Martyr*. Vol. 6, *The Fathers of the Church*. Washington, DC: Catholic University of America Press, 1948.

Life of Adam and Eve. Translated by M. D. Johnson. Vol. 2, *The Old Testament Pseudepigrapha*. Edited by James H. Charlesworth. Garden City, NY: Doubleday, 1985.

Methodius. *From the Discourse on the Resurrection*. Vol. 6, *Ante-Nicene Fathers*. Reprint. Peabody, MA: Hendrickson, 1999.

Migne, J. P., editor. *Patrologia Graeca*. 166 vols. Paris: : Migne, 1857–66.

———, editor. *Patrologia Latina*. 221 vols. Paris: Migne, 1844–64.

Origen, *Commentari Romanos*, Rom. 5.12, Col. 1029. Vol. 24, *Patrologia Latinia*, edited by J. P. Migne. Paris: Migne, 1844–64.

Theophilus to Autolycus. Vol. 2, *Ante-Nicene Fathers*. Reprint. Peabody, MA: Hendrickson, 1999.

Tertullian. *A Treatise on the Soul*. Vol. 3, *Ante-Nicene Fathers*. Reprint. Peabody, MA: Hendrickson, 1999.

———. *Against Hermonogenes*. Vol. 3, *Ante-Nicene Fathers*. Reprint. Peabody, MA: Hendrickson, 1999.

———. *Against Marcion*. Vol. 3, *Ante-Nicene Fathers*. Reprint. Peabody, MA: Hendrickson, 1999.

———. *On Baptism*. Vol. 3, *Ante-Nicene Fathers*. Reprint. Peabody, MA: Hendrickson, 1999.

———. *The Soul's Testimony*. Vol. 3, *Ante-Nicene Fathers*. Reprint. Peabody, MA: Hendrickson, 1999.

2 *(Syriac Apocalypse of) Baruch)*. Translated by A. J. Klijn. Vol. 1, *The Old Testament Pseudepigrapha*. Edited by James H. Charlesworth. Garden City, NY: Doubleday, 1985.

Vermes, Geza. *The Complete Dead Sea Scrolls in English*. New York: Penguin, 1998.

SECONDARY SOURCES

Adams, Edward. *Constructing the World: A Study of Paul's Cosmological Language*. Edinburgh: T. & T. Clark, 2000.

Anderson, Gary A. *Sin: A History*. New Haven: Yale University Press, 2009.

Arbel, Daphna, J. R. C. Cousland, Dietmar Neufeld. . . . *"And So They Went Out." The Lives of Adam and Eve as Cultural Transformative Stories*. London: T. & T. Clark, 2010.

Attridge, Harold W. "Sin, Sinners." In *New Interpreters Dictionary of the Bible*, Vol. 5, edited by Katherine D. Sakenfeld, 263–79. Nashville: Abingdon, 2009.

Barr, James. *The Garden of Eden and the Hope of Immortality*. Minneapolis: Fortress, 1993.

Beker, J. Christian. *Paul's Apocalyptic Gospel: The Coming Triumph of God*. Philadelphia: Fortress, 1982.

———. *Paul the Apostle: The Triumph of God in Life and Thought*. Philadelphia: Fortress, 1980.

———. *The Triumph of God: The Essence of Paul's Thought*. Minneapolis: Fortress, 1990.

Biddle, Mark E. *Missing the Mark: Sin and Its Consequences in Biblical Theology*. Nashville: Abingdon, 2005.

Bird, Michael, and Preston M. Sprinkle, editors. *The Faith of Jesus Christ*. Milton Keynes, UK: Paternoster, 2009.

Bloesch, Donald G. *Essentials of Evangelical Theology*. 2 vols. San Francisco: Harper and Row, 1978.

Blowers, Paul M. "Original Sin." In *Encyclopedia of Early Christianity*, vol. 2, 2nd ed., edited by Everett Ferguson, 839–40. New York: Garland, 1997.

Boccaccini, Gabriele. *Beyond the Essene Hypothesis: The Parting of the Ways between Qumran and Enochic Judaism*. Grand Rapids: Eerdmans, 1998.

Bonaiuti, Ernesto. "The Genesis of St. Augustine's Idea of Original Sin." *Harvard Theological Review* 10 (1917) 159–75.

Bonhoeffer, Dietrich. *Creation and Fall: A Theological Exposition of Genesis 1–3*. Vol. 3, *Dietrich Bonhoeffer Works*. Minneapolis: Fortress, 1997.

Bonner, Gerald. "Augustine on Romans 5.12." In *Studia Evangelica*, Vol. 5, edited by Frank L. Cross, 242–47. Berlin: Akademie, 1968.

———. *St. Augustine of Hippo*. Philadelphia: Westminster, 1963.

Bouteneff, Peter C. *Beginnings: Ancient Christian Readings of the Biblical Creation Narratives*. Grand Rapids: Baker Academic, 2008.

Bray, Gerald. "Original Sin in Patristic Thought." *Churchman* 108 (1994) 37–47.

———, editor. *Romans*. Ancient Christian Commentary on Scripture. Downers Grove, IL: InterVarsity, 1998.

Brown, Alexandra R. *The Cross and Human Transformation: Paul's Apocalyptic Word in 1 Corinthians*. Minneapolis: Fortress, 1989.

Brown, Derek, R. "The Devil in the Details: A Survey of Research on Satan in Biblical Studies." *Currents in Biblical Research* 9 (2000) 200–227.

Brown, Peter. *Augustine of Hippo*. Berkeley: University of California Press, 1967.

———. *The Body and Society. Men, Women and Sexual Renunciation in Early Christianity*. New York: Columbia University Press, 1988.

Bruggemann, Walter. *Introduction to the Old Testament*. Louisville: Westminster/John Knox, 2003.

Bryan, Christopher. *A Preface to Romans*. Oxford: Oxford University Press, 2000.

Burns, J. Patout. "Traducianism." In *Encyclopedia of Early Christianity*, vol. 2, 2nd ed., edited by Everett Ferguson, 1141. New York: Garland, 1997.

Byrne, Brendan. *Romans*. Sacra Pagina. Collegeville, MN: Liturgical, 1996.

Carpenter, Eugene and Michael A. Grisanti. "פשׁע (pesa)." In *New International Dictionary of Old Testament Theology and Exegesis*, Vol. 3, edited by Willem A. Van Gemeren, 706–10. Grand Rapids: Zondervan, 1997.

Carter, T. L. *Paul and the Power of Sin: Redefining "Beyond the Pale."* SNTMS 115. Cambridge: Cambridge University Press, 2002.

Chadwick, Henry. *The Church in Ancient Society*. Oxford: Oxford University Press, 2001.

Chazon, Esther Glickler. "The Creation and Fall of Adam in the Dead Sea Scrolls." In *The Book of Genesis in Jewish and Oriental Christian Interpretation*, edited by Judith Frishman and Lucas van Rompay, 11–24. Leuven: Peeters, 1997.

Clendenin, Daniel B. *Eastern Orthodox Christianity: A Western Perspective*. Grand Rapids: Baker, 1994.

Collins, John J. "Before the Fall: The Earliest Interpretations of Adam and Eve." In *The Idea of Biblical Interpretation: Essays in Honor of James L. Kugel*, edited by H. Najman and J. H. Newman, 293–308. Leiden: Brill, 2004.

———. *Jewish Wisdom in the Hellenistic Age*. Old Testament Library. Louisville: Westminister/John Knox, 1997.

———. *The Apocalyptic Imagination*. New York: Crossroads, 1987.

———. "The Origin of Evil in Apocalyptic Literature and the Dead Sea Scrolls." In *Seers, Sybils and Sages in Hellenistic-Roman Judaism*, 287–99. New York: Brill, 1997.

Collins, Raymond F. *First Corinthians*. Sacra Pagina. Collegeville MN: Liturgical, 1999.

———. *1 and 2 Timothy and Titus*. New Testament Library. Louisville: Westminster/ John Knox, 2002.

Confession of Faith in a Mennonite Perspective. Scottdale, PA: Herald, 1995.

Confession of Faith of the US and Canadian Conferences of the Mennonite Brethren Churches. Winnipeg, MB: Kindred, 1999.

Cranfield, C. E. B. *The Epistle to the Romans*. 2 vols. International Critical Commentary. Edinburgh: T. & T. Clark, 1975, 1979.

Davidson, M. J. *Angels at Qumran. A Comparative Study of 1 Enoch 1–36, 72–108 and the Sectarian Writings from Qumran*. Sheffield, UK: JSOT, 1992.

de Boer, Martinus C. *The Defeat of Death: Apocalyptic Eschatology in 1 Corinthians 15 and Romans 5*. JSNTS Supplements 22. Sheffield, UK: Sheffield Academic Press, 1988.

de Jonge, M., and J. Tromp. *The Life of Adam and Eve and Related Literature*. Guides to Apocrypha and Pseudepigrapha 4. Sheffield, UK: Sheffield Academic Press, 1997.

De Simone, Russell J. "Modern Research on the Sources of Saint Augustine's Doctrine of Original Sin." *Augustinian Studies* 11 (1980) 205–27.

Downing, Victor K. "The Doctrine of Regeneration in the Second Century." *Evangelical Review of Theology* 14 (1990) 99–112.

Dueck, Al. "Speaking the Languages of Sin and Pathology." *Christian Counseling Today* 10 (2002) 20–21.

Dunn, James D. G. *Romans*. Word Biblical Commentary. 2 vols. Dallas: Word, 1988.

Dyck, Cornelius U. "Sinners and Saints." In *A Legacy of Faith*, edited by C. J. Dyck, 87–102. Newton, KS: Faith and Life, 1962.

Easter, Matthew E. "The *Pistis Christou* Debate: Main Arguments and Responses in Summary." *Currents in Biblical Research* 9 (2010) 33–47.

Ellis, Teresa Ann, "Is Eve the 'Woman' in Sirach 25.24?" *Catholic Biblical Quarterly* 73 (2011) 723–42.

Ferguson, Everett. *Baptism in the Early Church*. Grand Rapids: Eerdmans, 2009.

Finger, Thomas. *Christian Theology. An Eschatological Approach*. 2 vols. Scottdale, PA: Herald, 1985.

Fitzmyer, Joseph A. "The Consecutive Meaning of EPH' HO in Romans 5.12." *New Testament Studies* 39 (1993) 321–39.

———. *Romans*. Anchor Bible. New York: Doubleday, 1972.

Fredricksen, Paula. "Beyond the Body/Soul Dichotomy." *Recherches Augustiniennes* 23 (1988) 87–114.

———. *Sin. The Early History of an Idea*. Princeton: Princeton University Press, 2012.

Fretheim, Terrence E. "The Book of Genesis." The New Interpreters Bible, Vol. 1. Nashville: Abingdon, 1994.

———. *God and the World in the Old Testament: A Relational Theology of Creation*. Nashville: Abingdon, 2005.

———. "Is Genesis 3 a Fall Story?" *Word & Word* XIV (Spring 1994) 144–53.

Friedman, Robert. "The Doctrine of Original Sin as Held by the Anabaptists of the Sixteenth Century." *Mennonite Quarterly Review* 33 (1959) 206–14.

Furnish, Victor Paul. *II Corinthians*. Anchor Bible. Garden City, NY: Doubleday, 1984.

Gaventa, Beverly Roberts. "Interpreting the Death of Jesus Apocalyptically: Reconsidering Romans 8.32." In *Jesus and Paul Reconsidered*, edited by Todd D. Still, 125–45. Grand Rapids: Eerdmans, 2007.

Goldingay, John. *Old Testament Theology. Vol. 1: Israel's Gospel.* Downers Grove, IL: InterVarsity, 2003.

Gonzalez, Justo L. *Christian Thought Revisited: Three Types of Theology.* Nashville: Abingdon, 1989.

Graves, Joseph L. *The Emperor's New Clothes: Biological Theories of Race at the Millennium.* Piscataway, NJ: Rutgers University Press, 2001.

Green, Joel B. *Body, Soul, and Human Life: The Nature of Humanity in the Bible.* Grand Rapids: Baker Academic, 2008.

Grenz, Stanley J. *Theology for the Community of God.* Nashville: Broadman and Holman, 1994.

Grudem, Wayne. *Systematic Theology: An Introduction to Biblical Doctrine.* Grand Rapids: Zondervan, 1994.

Guenther, W. "Sin." In *New International Dictionary of New Testament Theology*, Vol. 3, edited by Colin Brown, 573–85. Grand Rapids: Zondervan, 1978.

Hamilton, Victor P. *The Book of Genesis 1–17.* International Commentary on the Old Testament. Grand Rapids: Eerdmans, 1990.

Harris, Murray J. *The Second Epistle to the Corinthians.* New International Greek New Testament Commentary. Grand Rapids: Eerdmans, 2005.

Hays, Richard. *First Corinthians.* Interpretation. Louisville: John Knox, 1997.

Hogan, Katrina Martin. "The Exegetical Background of the 'Ambiguity of Death' in the Wisdom of Solomon." *Journal for the Study of Judaism* 30 (1999) 1–24.

Hoffman, Lawrence A. "Principle, Story, and Myth in the Liturgical Search for Identity." *Interpretation* 64 (2010) 231–45.

Jewett, Robert. *Romans.* Heremenia. Minneapolis: Fortress, 2007.

Johnson, Timothy Luke. *Letters to Paul's Delegates.* Valley Forge, PA: Trinity, 1996.

———. *The Writings of the New Testament.* Minneapolis: Fortress, 1999.

Kasujja, Augustine. *Polygenism and the Theology of Original Sin Today.* Rome: Urbaniana University Press, 1986.

Kaufmann, Richard A., "Sin." In *The Mennonite Encyclopedia*, Vol. 5, edited by Cornelius J. Dyck and Dennis M. Martin, 821–25. Scottdale, PA: Herald, 1990.

Keeney, William. *The Development of Dutch Anabaptist Thought and Practice from 1539–1564.* Nieuwkoop: De Graaf, 1968.

Kelly, Henry Ansgar. *Satan: A Biography.* Cambridge: Cambridge University Press, 2006.

Kelly, J. N. D. *Early Christian Doctrines.* New York: Harper and Row, 1978.

Kepnes, Steven. "Sin and Repentance." In *Christianity in Jewish Terms*, edited by Tikva Frymer-Kensky, David Novak, Peter Ochs, David Fox Sandmel, Michael A. Signer, 293–304. Boulder, CO: Westview, 2000.

Knierim, Rolf. *Die Hauptbegriffe für Sünde im Alten Testament.* Guetersloh: Mohn, 1965.

Koch, Klaus. "אטח (chata)." In *Theological Dictionary of the Old Testament*, Vol. IV, edited by G. Johannes Botterweck and Helmer Ringgren, 309–19. Grand Rapids: Eerdmans, 1980.

Kugel, James L. *Traditions of the Bible: A Guide to the Bible As It Was at the Start of the Common Era.* Cambridge: Harvard University Press, 1998.

Kuhn, K. G. "Die Sektenschrift und die iranische Religion." *Zeitschrift für Theologie und Kirche* 49 (1952) 296–316.

Lambrecht, Jan. *Second Corinthians.* Sacra Pagina. Collegeville, MN: Liturgical, 1999.

Landes, Paula Fredricksen. *Augustine on Romans: Propositions from the Epistle to the Romans: Unfinished Commentary on the Epistle to the Romans.* Chico, CA: Scholars, 1982.

Leith, John H. *Creeds of the Church.* Garden City, NY: Doubleday, 1963.

Levison, John R. *Portraits of Adam in Early Judaism: From Sirach to 2 Baruch.* JSP Supplement Series 1. Sheffield, UK: Sheffield Academic Press, 1988.

————. "The Two Spirits in Qumran Theology." In *The Bible and the Dead Sea Scrolls,* edited by James H. Charlesworth, 169–94. The Dead Sea Scrolls and the Qumran Community, Vol. 2. Waco, TX: Baylor University Press, 2006.

Levison, Jack. "Is Eve to Blame? A Contextual Analysis of Sirach 25.24." *Catholic Biblical Quarterly* 47 (1985) 617–23.

Livingston, David N. *Adam's Ancestors: Race, Religion and the Politics of Human Origins.* Baltimore: John Hopkins University Press, 2008.

Loewen, Howard John. *One Lord, One Church, One Hope and One God. Mennonite Confessions of Faith in North America.* Elkhart, IN: Institute of Mennonite Studies, 1985.

Luc, Alex. "עָוֹן (awon)." In *New International Dictionary of Old Testament Theology and Exegesis,* Vol. 3, edited by Willem A. Van Gemeren, 351. Grand Rapids: Zondervan, 1997.

————. "אטה (ht)." In *New International Dictionary of Old Testament Theology and Exegesis,* Vol. 2, edited by Willem A. Van Gemeren, 87–93. Grand Rapids: Zondervan, 1997.

Lunn-Rockliffe, Sophie, *Ambrosiaster's Political Theology.* Oxford Early Christian Studies. Oxford: Oxford University Press, 2007.

McClendon, James Wm. *Systematic Theology. Vol. 2: Doctrine.* Nashville: Abingdon, 1994.

McFadyen, Alistair. *Bound to Sin: Abuse, Holocaust and the Christian Doctrine of Sin.* Cambridge: Cambridge University Press, 2000.

McWilliam, Joanne. "Pelagius, Pelagianism." In *Encylopedia of Early Christianity,* Vol. 2, 2nd ed., edited by Everett Ferguson, 887–90. New York: Garland, 1997.

Mann, William E. "Augustine on Evil and Original Sin." In *The Cambridge Companion to Augustine,* edited by Eleonore Stump and Norman Kretzmann, 40–48. Cambridge: Cambridge University Press, 2001.

Marpeck, Pilgrim. *The Writings of Pilgrim Marpeck.* Translated by William Klassen and Walter Klaassen. Scottdale, PA: Herald, 1978.

Marshall, I. Howard, and Philip H. Towner. *The Pastoral Epistles.* The International Critical and Exegetical Commentary. Edinburgh: T. & T. Clark, 1999.

Martens, E. A. "Sin, Guilt." In *Dictionary of the Old Testament Pentateuch,* edited by T. Desmond Alexander and David W. Baker, 764–78. Downers Grove, IL: InterVarsity, 2003.

Martin, Ralph P. *2 Corinthians.* Word Biblical Commentary. Waco, TX: Word, 1986.

Meyendorff, John. *Byzantine Theology.* New York: Fordham University Press, 1979.

Mitchell, Margaret M. *The Heavenly Trumpet: John Chrysostom and the Art of Pauline Interpretation.* Louisville: Westminster/John Knox, 2002.

Neenan, William B. "Doctrine of Original Sin in Scripture." *Irish Theological Quarterly* 28 (1961) 54–64.

Nickelsburg, George W. E. *Ancient Judaism and Christian Origins.* Minneapolis, Fortress, 2003.

———. *Jewish Literature between the Bible and the Mishnah*. Philadelphia: Fortress, 1981.

O'Donnell, James J. *Augustine: A New Biography*. New York: Harper Perennial, 2005.

Pagels, Elaine. *Adam, Eve, and the Serpent*. New York: Vintage, 1989.

Pelikan, Jaroslav, and Valerie Hotchkis, editors. *Creeds and Confessions in the Christian Tradition*. 4 vols. New Haven: Yale University Press, 2003.

Pelikan, Jaroslav. *The Christian Tradition: A History of the Development of Doctrine*. Vol. 1, *The Emergence of the Catholic Tradition, 100–600*. Chicago: University of Chicago, 1971.

Plantinga, Jr., Cornelius. *Not the Way It's Supposed to Be: A Breviary of Sin*. Grand Rapids: Eerdmans, 1995.

Quasten, Johannes. *Patrology*. 3 vols. Utrecht-Antwerp: Spectrum, 1975.

Quell, Gottfried, Georg Bertram, Gustav Staehlin, Walter Grundmann. "*hamartano.*" In *Theological Dictionary of the New Testament*, Vol. 1, edited by Gerhard Kittel, 267–316. Grand Rapids: Eerdmans, 1964.

Rigby, Paul. "Original Sin." In *Augustine through the Ages: An Encyclopedia*, edited by Allan D. Fitzgerald, 607–14. Grand Rapids: Eerdmans, 1999.

———. *Original Sin in Augustine's Confessions*. Ottawa, ON: University of Ottawa Press, 1987.

Rist, John M. *Augustine*. Cambridge: Cambridge University Press, 1994.

Rondet, Henri. *Original Sin: The Patristic and Theological Background*. Shannon, Ireland: Ecclesia, 1972.

Rubinkiewicz, R. "Apocalypse of Abraham." In *The Old Testament Pseudepigrapha*, Vol. 1, edited by James H. Charlesworth, 681–705. Garden City, NY: Doubleday, 1983.

Russell, Jeffrey Burton. *The Devil: Perceptions of Evil from Antiquity to Primitive Christianity*. Ithaca, NY: Cornell University Press, 1977.

Sanders, E. P. "Sin, Sinners." In *Anchor Bible Dictionary*, Vol. 6, edited by David N. Freedman, 31–47. New York: Doubleday, 1992.

Sandmel, Samuel. "Parallelomania." *Journal of Biblical Literature* 81 (1962) 1–13.

Sauer, Eric. *The Dawn of World Redemption*. Grand Rapids: Eerdmans, 1951.

Scroggs, Robin. *The Last Adam*. Minneapolis: Fortress, 1966.

Skehan, Patrick W., and Alexander A. DiLella. *The Wisdom of Ben Sira*. Anchor Bible. New York: Doubleday, 1987.

Souter, Alexander. *The Earliest Latin Commentaries on the Epistles of St. Paul*. Oxford: Clarendon, 1927.

———. *Pelagius' Expositions of the Thirteen Epistles of St. Paul*. Cambridge Texts and Studies, IX. Vol. 1, Introduction. Vol. 2, Text. Cambridge: University of Cambridge Press, 1922, 1926.

———. *A Study of Ambrosiaster*. Cambridge Texts and Studies, Vol. VII. Cambridge: Cambridge University Press, 1905.

Steenberg, M. C. "Children in Paradise: Adam and Eve as 'Infants' in Irenaeus of Lyons." *Journal of Early Christian Studies* 12 (2004) 10–22.

Stendahl, Krister. "The Apostle Paul and the Introspective Conscience of the West." *Paul among Jews and Gentiles*, 78–96. Philadelphia: Fortress, 1976.

Stokes, Ryan E. "The Origin of Sin in the Dead Sea Scrolls." *Southwestern Journal of Theology* 53 (2010) 55–67.

Stone, Michael E. *Fourth Ezra*. Hermeneia. Minneapolis: Fortress, 1990.

———. *A History of the Literature of Adam and Eve*. Early Judaism and Its Literature 3. Atlanta: Scholars, 1992.

Strong, Augustus H. *Systematic Theology*. Philadelphia: Judson, 1907.

Stuckenbruck, Loren T. "The Interiorization of Dualism within the Human Being in Second Temple Judaism: The Treatise of the Two Spirits (1QS III.13—IV.26) in Its Tradition-Historical Context." In *Light against Darkness: Dualism in Ancient Mediterranean Religion and the Contemporary World*, edited by Armin Lange, et al., 145–68. Gottingen: Vandenhoeck & Ruprecht, 2011.

Taylor, Barbara Brown. *Speaking of Sin: The Lost Language of Salvation*. Cambridge, MA: Cowley, 2000.

Tennant, F. R. *The Sources of the Doctrines of the Fall and Original Sin*. 1903. Reprint. New York: Schocken, 1946.

Thiselton, Anthony C. *The Living Paul*. Downers Grove, IL: InterVarsity, 2009.

Thompson, Alden, Lloyd. *Responsibility for Evil in the Theodicy of IV Ezra*. Missoula, MT: Scholars, 1977.

Toews, John E. "Righteousness in Romans: The Political Subtext of Paul's Letter." In *The Old Testament in the Life of God's People*, edited by Jon Isaak, 209–22. Winona Lake, IN: Eisenbrauns, 2009.

———. *Romans*. Believers Church Bible Commentary. Scottdale, PA: Herald, 2004.

Towner, Philip H. *The Letters to Timothy and Titus*. New International Commentary on the New Testament. Grand Rapids: Eerdmans, 2006.

Trible, Phyllis. *God and the Rhetoric of Sexuality*. Philadelphia: Fortress, 1978.

Urbach, Ephraim E. *The Sages: Their Concepts and Beliefs*. Jerusalem: Magnes, 1975.

van Oyen, Geert. "The Character of Eve in the New Testament: 2 Corinthians 11.3 and 2 Timothy 2.13–14." In *Out of Paradise: Eve and Adam and Their Interpreters*, edited by Bob Becking and Susan Hennecke, 14–28. Sheffield, UK: Sheffield Phoenix, 2010.

Vermes, Geza. "Genesis 1–3 in Post-Biblical Hebrew and Aramaic Literature before the Mishnah." *Journal of Jewish Studies* 43 (1992), 221–25.

von Rad, Gerhard. *Genesis*. Old Testament Library. Philadelphia: Westminster, 1972.

Vawter, Bruce. *On Genesis: A New Reading*. Garden City, NY: Doubleday, 1977.

Ware, Timothy. *The Orthodox Church*. New York: Penguin, 1997.

Weaver, David. "The Exegesis of Romans 5.12 among the Greek Fathers and Its Implications for the Doctrine of Original Sin: The 5th–12th Centuries." *St. Vladimir's Theological Quarterly* 27 (1985) 133–59.

———. "From Paul to Augustine: Romans 5.12 in Early Christian Exegesis." *St. Vladimir's Theological Quarterly* 27 (1983) 187–206.

Weaver, Rebecca H. "Anthroplogy." In *Encyclopedia of Early Christianity*, Vol. 1, 2nd ed., edited by Everett Ferguson, 60–65. New York: Garland, 1997.

Weingart, Richard E. "The Meaning of Sin in the Theology of Menno Simons." *Mennonite Quarterly Review* 41 (1967) 25–39.

Wenham, Gordon, J. *Genesis 1–15*. Word Biblical Commentary. Waco, TX: Word, 1987.

Westermann, Claus. *Genesis*. Interpretation. Atlanta: John Knox, 1982.

———. *Genesis 1–11*. Minneapolis: Augsburg, 1984.

Wiley, Tatha. *Original Sin*. New York: Paulist, 2002.

Williams, Norman Powell. *The Ideas of the Fall and of Original Sin*. Bampton Lectures 1924. New York: Longmans, Green and Co., 1927.

Bibliography

Wingren, Gustaf. *Man and the Incarnation: A Study in the Biblical Theology of Irenaeus.* Philadelphia: Muhlenberg, 1947.

Winston, David. "Philo's Doctrine of Free Will." In *Two Treatises of Philo of Alexandria,* edited by David Winston and John Dillon, 181–95. Chico, CA: Scholars, 1983.

Witherington, Ben. *Conflict and Community in Corinth.* Grand Rapids: Eerdmans, 1995.

Wright, David F. "Augustine and the Transformation of Baptism." In *The Origins of Christendom in the West,* edited by Alan Kreider, 287–310. Edinburgh: T. & T. Clark, 2001.

Wright, N. T. "Adam in Pauline Christology." In *Society of Biblical Literature Seminar Papers, 1983,* edited by Kent H. Richard, 359–89. Chico, CA: Scholars, 1983.

———. *The Climax of the Covenant.* Minneapolis: Fortress, 1991.

———. *Paul.* Minneapolis: Fortress, 2005.

Zoloth, Laurie. "Exile and Return in a World of Injustice: A Response to Steven Kepnes." In *Christianity in Jewish Terms,* edited by Tikva Frymer-Kensky et al., 305–12. Boulder, CO: Westview, 2000.

Subject Index

Scripture Index

2 Peter

2:5	94
3:7	94

Jude

4	94
15	94
18	94

24750434R00081

Printed in Great Britain
by Amazon